ELITE ATTACK FORCES

WAFFEN-SS 2

ELITE ATTACK FORCES

WAFFEN-SS 2

Patrick Hook,
Michael Sharpe and
Brian L. Davis

CHARTWELL
BOOKS, INC.

This edition published by 2007 by

CHARTWELL BOOKS,
A Division of
BOOK SALES, INC.
114 Northfield Avenue
Edison, New Jersey 08837

ISBN: 978-1-84013-828-3

© 2007 Compendium Publishing Ltd, 43 Frith Street, London, W1D 4SA
Previously published in the Spearhead series

Cataloging-in-Publication data is available from the Library of Congress

Printed in China through Printworks Int. Ltd

Acknowledgements
Photographs via TRH Pictures, Simon Dunstan (where credited), Brian L. Davis, and Ray Bonds.

Previous page: Hohenstaufen PzKpfw IV Ausf H in France during 1944.

CONTENTS

HOHENSTAUFEN
9th SS Panzer Division

Patrick Hook

ORIGINS & HISTORY

On New Year's Eve 1942, Hitler agreed to the formation of two new divisions for the Waffen-SS. These were the 9th and 10th SS Panzergrenadier Divisions. The 9th was later given the name *Hohenstaufen*, and its sister, the 10th, became *Frundsberg*. Formed in 1943, *Hohenstaufen* was given the number 9 simply because it was the ninth division to be created in the Waffen-SS. The name Hohenstaufen was a homage to one of Germany's ancient noble families, a dynasty of the Holy Roman Empire which provided several kings and emperors between the years 1138 and 1254. The earliest known head of the family was Emperor Friedrich Barbarossa, the Count of Buren, who died in 1094. His son, Friedrich II, built a castle at Staufen near Lorsch in Swabia which was called Hohenstaufen; he later changed his surname to that of his castle. Friedrich II was one of Hitler's favourite historical personalities, and it is believed this was why the family name was used for the 9th Panzer Division. Both Friedrichs are of particular importance to German history but Barbarossa — as with Arthur in British myth and legend — is said to be sleeping in the mountains awaiting Germany's direst need.

Below: Friedrich (Frederick) I Barbarossa (c.1123–90), Holy Roman Emperor, King of Germany and Italy: he and his grandson Frederick II were the greatest of the Hohenstaufens under whom German culture and power waxed strong. They were favourites of Hitler and the Nazis — as was shown, of course, by the codename for the invasion of Russia.

The SS or *Schutzstaffel* was originally formed as Hitler's personal protection unit in 1925. One of its main roles was to take care of internal German security, and in line with the Nazi political ideal, in the early days it only took true Aryan candidates. As time went on and manpower became shorter, however, this rule was relaxed. The Waffen-SS was formed by Heinrich Himmler in December 1940, when it was created out of the *Leibstandarte*, the *SS-Verfügungstruppe* and the *Totenkopf Standarten* as a third branch of the SS. It represented the true military part of this large and politically complex organisation, and while it was initially intended to act as security for the homeland, it was not long before Hitler ordered his elite to the front line.

The other two parts of the SS were the *Allgemeine-SS* (General SS) which served a political and administrative role, and the *SS-Totenkopfverband* (SS Death's Head Organisation). Hitler put his own men in to command the Waffen-SS as he had fallen out with many of the regular army's high-class senior officers who saw him as an uncultured upstart. As a result he wanted his new SS army to become the military's elite formation, and so he heavily favoured it with all the best troops and equipment. He also ensured that the Waffen-SS retained strategic control over its actions, although it did come under the day to day tactical control of the OKW (*Oberkommando der Wehrmacht*). In many of the biggest conflicts of the war the Waffen-SS played a major role — either leading the way into battle or, as the tide turned against the Nazis, holding furious rearguard actions to help other units get away to safety. By the end of the war the Waffen-SS numbered nearly 600,000 men, although at one time it reached a peak of 900,000 ranged over 41 divisions. Around half of these were non-Germans who had been recruited either as volunteers or by force.

Although some of the SS units perpetrated atrocities on civilians or prisoners, this was by no means the case for all of them. *Hohenstaufen* troops, for instance, are not recorded as ever having committed any such acts and, indeed, were commended for their good treatment of Allied prisoners at Arnhem.

When the 9th and 10th divisions were first formed they were designated as mechanised infantry (*Panzergrenadier*) divisions rather than as full armoured (*Panzer*) divisions, although technically they had sufficient armour to qualify. At this early stage neither had been assigned their famous names — they were simply referred to by their divisional numbers. For the SS to decide to form new divisions was one thing, but finding sufficient recruits to man them was quite another. The German armed forces had been fighting in one form or another for seven years, and after the massive losses incurred on the Eastern Front, there were few men of the right ages available. Due to the severe shortage of manpower, the SS forced large numbers of people to 'volunteer'. Somewhere in the region of 70 percent of them were 18-year old conscripts from the RAD — the *Reichsarbeitsdienst* (National Labour Service). This had been formed by the NSDAP as the official national labour union since those in existence during World War I had been a hotbed of communism and other left-wing political activism. They had wrought havoc in many places such as the dockyards of Hamburg and Kiel, and as they were considered to pose a threat to the country, they were declared illegal.

The young men drafted into the RAD had to do manual labour for at least three months; during this time they often had to live in rudimentary conditions with harsh discipline. For some this meant acting as virtual slave labour on farms, whereas others worked in urban areas doing things like digging air raid shelters or helping with municipal projects. Although the RAD was ostensibly a labour union, it was effectively a conduit straight into the armed forces. In many ways it provided a valuable pre-military training for young civilians — this undoubtedly helped speed up their conversion into trained soldiers.

The first 9th Division cadres were formed at the LSSAH (*Leibstandarte-SS* Adolf Hitler) Replacement Battalion in Berlin-Lichterfelde in January 1943; these consisted of a basic staff and training units. In order to help turn the division into a fighting force, experienced men were brought in from the *Leibstandarte*; they formed the division's core, and trained the newly inducted recruits. The division's numbers were also swelled by ethnic Germans, many of whom came from Hungary.

In early February 1943, enough troops had been assembled for the division to move to a training area or *Truppenübungsplatz*, at Mailly-le-Camp. This was to the east of Paris, between Chalons-sur-Marne and Troyes. The division moved out on 8 February, and a few days later SS-Brigadeführer und Generalmajor der Waffen-SS Wilhelm ('Willi') Bittrich took command over the division under Armeegruppe D, OKW. He ensured that the raw recruits underwent all manner of combat training, including against airborne assaults, a feature that helped them immensely at Arnhem.

The 9th SS Panzergrenadier Division *Hohenstaufen* was officially given the name *Hohenstaufen* on 19 March 1943, and at the same time the men were given their cuff-bands (see page 75), of which they became very proud. After undergoing further training, *Hohenstaufen* was put under the command of the Fifteenth Armee and moved north to the Ypres area. The next month the division was moved again, this time to Amiens to take over an army camp vacated by a departing armoured division; it continued training there until the end of the year.

On 23 October 1943, the 9th SS-Panzergrenadier Division *Hohenstaufen* was renamed the 9th SS Panzer Division *Hohenstaufen*, and put under IV SS Panzerkorps*; the new assignment was formalised three days later on 26 October. At the same time the division's two infantry regiments were redesignated from the 1st and 2nd to the 19th

Above: The Hohenstaufen family crest.

* It can be difficult to differentiate between Allied and Axis unit designations in a book of this nature because words such as division or regiment are spelled the same way in German and English. To aid clarity, throughout this book we have used the German spellings for corps (Korps) and army (Armee).

and 20th. The division also took delivery of a consignment of new PzKpfw V Panther tanks, and its order of battle was reorganised. The changes included the addition of a battery of artillery (although this did not arrive for some time).

On 12 November the division's 15th Motorcycle Company and 2nd Infantry Regiment were detached and assigned to the Reconnaissance Unit (*Aufklärungs-Abteilung*) of the new 16th SS Panzergrenadier Division *Reichsführer-SS*. At the same time the anti-aircraft company (*Flak-Kompanie*) and a survey troop (*Messbatterie*) were also moved elsewhere. The division spent December 1943 as a reserve force under Fifteenth Army, Armeegruppe D, and then was put under I SS-Panzerkorps in January 1944.

In mid-February *Hohenstaufen* was moved south to the Nimes/Avignon area, not far north of the Mediterranean coast. It took over from the Panzer Lehr Division (Tank Demonstration Division), and underwent the last few weeks of its training before becoming a front-line combat unit. When this ended, together with sister division *Frundsberg, Hohenstaufen* was put under II SS-Panzerkorps, headed by Paul Hausser, as part of the OKW reserve.

The II SS-Panzerkorps had been formed in June 1942 before it was transferred to France to take over the Waffen-SS divisions being refitted there. In January 1943 it was moved to the southern part of the Eastern Front, where it fought at Kharkov and Belgorod and then became part of the summer offensive. When it looked as though Mussolini was going to be deposed, the Panzerkorps was transferred to Italy. It was moved to France in December 1943, and then back to the Eastern Front in April 1944. Shortly after this it was sent back to France to help fight the Allies after the invasion of Normandy. After this it took part in the Ardennes Offensive, and then returned to the Eastern Front once again. The unit ended its war in Austria.

Below: Waffen-SS troops in house-to-house fighting on the Eastern Front. By the end of the war there would be 38 Waffen-SS divisions (although some were divisions only in name and never had the requisite strength or weapons), a number of them — such as *Wiking* and *Nordland* — using foreign volunteers. In 1940 there were only 100,000 men in the Waffen-SS: at its peak it would number over 900,000 and in 1943–44 its armoured units would control a quarter of the tanks available to the German ground forces.

READY FOR WAR

RECRUITMENT

When the SS first began recruiting for new blood, due to the patriotic fervour whipped up by Hitler they had the pick of an extremely large crop of enthusiastic nationals. As a result of this abundance of men, their standards were extremely high. The basic requirements were that anyone seeking to join would have to be between 17 and 22 years old and be at least 168cm (5ft 9in) tall (this was set as it was Himmler's height). They also had to have no criminal record and be able to demonstrate a pure Aryan descent as far back as 1800 for enlisted men and 1750 for officers. They had to sign up for different terms of service depending on their rank — this was a minimum of four years for enlisted men, 12 years for NCOs and 25 years for officers. During the 1930s the pass rate was only 15 percent — to some extent because Himmler personally vetted photographs of all the officer candidates to ensure that they all looked sufficiently racially pure.

By 1943, it was clear that large numbers of recruits were needed to keep the Waffen-SS fully manned. As a result there was a massive recruiting drive among various nationalities and ethnic groups that would not have been considered to meet the SS racial purity standard. In order to encourage them to sign up, the standards were also lowered. The new intake of recruits only had to sign up for two years or the duration of war; they did not have to join the SS, and only had to be able to pass the lowest of military standards. Foreign recruits were given variations of the usual SS insignia which they wore on their uniforms to indicate that they were of non-German origin.

During World War II around 922,000 soldiers served in the Waffen-SS; of these about 400,000 were Reich Germans, 137,000 were pure West Europeans, 200,000 were pure East Europeans and 185,000 were Volksdeutsche.

As time went on the recruitment standards slipped even further, and by mid-1944 more or less the only criterion was whether the candidate was able to fire a rifle. At this stage many of the recruits being accepted came from other units and services, including the Luftwaffe, Kriegsmarine, the Labour Service (RAD) and the Hitler Youth.

TRAINING

All SS recruits received three weeks' basic training, although in 1942 all parade ground training was stopped as it was not considered relevant for the battlefield. Further training then began — this was always extremely tough, and usually involved a strong element of inter-disciplinary education. The three main elements that the SS sought to develop were physical fitness, character training and weapons skills. Within this they fostered aggressiveness, initiative and self-reliance. To instil these factors new recruits had a rigid discipline imposed on them, and blind obedience was rewarded. Displaying total trust

Above and Right: The four *Ordensburgen* (Order Castles) of Krössinsee, Vogelsang, Sonthofen and Marienburg were intended to provide training for the elite of the Nazi Party. It was planned that students would spend a year in each of the castles and, after their training, take up positions in the higher echelons of the party. Vogelsang, in the Eifel Mountains near Belgium, was designed by Professor Clemens Klotz and building started in March 1934. There was a foundation ceremony in front of Robert Ley in September of that year. With accommodation for 1,000 'Junkers' — squires is the closest English equivalent — the school concentrated on sports and basic military training: all to no avail. War interrupted the Ordensburg concept and most of those involved entered military service. The Vogelsang complex was bombarded briefly (some of the damage can be seen in the photo at right) and then captured in early February 1945 by units of US 9th Infantry Division. Postwar it was used by NATO.

and loyalty was an integral part of being in the Waffen-SS, and this was nurtured from the first day. Trainees were encouraged to participate in physical activities, especially sports. In an effort to produce elite soldiers, much of the training focussed on battlefield skills such as marksmanship, camouflage techniques and navigation abilities.

The Waffen-SS training units were always looking for ways to improve their teaching methods. A good example of this was that the Panzer crews of the 12th SS-Panzer Division *Hitlerjugend* had to spend a week working in the MAN tank factories in Nuremberg. The idea was to give them a better understanding of how the tanks worked so that they would look after them more carefully and know more about how to repair them when necessary. The training officers were also very keen to get direct feedback from the front line to ensure that new troops would gain from the latest knowledge gleaned from fighting in new environments, climates or against new kinds of weapons or tactics.

Officer cadets were sent to an *SS-Junkerschule* — the main ones being at Bad Tölz and Braunschweig. These were overseen by the then-Oberführer Paul Hausser and by 1937 were producing more than 400 exceptionally well-trained officers a year. Although many foreign nationals were accepted into the SS in the later stages of the war, the officers remained predominantly German. Recruits to the other ranks were sent to various training camps, some of which were alongside regular army troops.

Political and ideological indoctrination was initially an important part of the SS training regime; however, it was never as successful as the senior levels of the hierarchy

Above: The SS had its own officer training schools (*Junkerschulen*) which were built at Braunschweig and Bad Tölz. Sports training was extremely important — fitness was seen as a significant factor in Waffen-SS training to improve stamina and endurance. This 1942 photograph shows young men at Bad Tölz. Note the SS sports vest with the centrally placed SS sports symbol.

Above: Waffen-SS Panzer IV Ausf Es on exercise. Produced from September 1940 to April 1941, Ausf E versions were involved in 'Barabarossa' but most had been lost by 1944.

would have liked. Many recruits maintained their own religious beliefs in private, but gave a public face of acceptance. As the war got underway, it soon became clear that military skills were more important than political ones, and with the exception of some of the more sinister elements of the SS, most of the ideological courses were abandoned. Life expectancy on the battlefront was, after all, only two months.

THE ORGANISATION OF THE GERMAN ARMY

The German Army was organised into a series of units that fitted together to form a coherent structure. At the highest level was the *Heeresgruppe*, or senior army group; this was made up of several *Armeegruppe(n)*, or army groups, and was the largest German military formation of World War II. The Heeresgruppe would usually be based on a particular geographical region, and could contain several hundred thousand men spread across hundreds of units.

The Armeegruppe was typically made up of two or three *Armee(n)*, or armies, and came under the command of the Heeresgruppe, but whereas it had a clearly defined status at the beginning of the war, as time went on its format became less rigid. The armies that made up an Armeegruppe were sometimes all-German, but were more usually made up of one German army alongside one or more allied armies. When this was the case the German Army generally had seniority over its foreign neighbours. As the war progressed and the tide turned in favour of the Allies, the Axis forces could not maintain their original numbers due to the massive losses they were experiencing. This meant that a unit designated as an Armee, which would normally be made up of several *Korps*, or corps, could in reality be as small as an individual corps. An Armee operated at the strategic level, and so would usually also have several other units attached to it: these could include reserves, training units or specialist formations. In all an Armee would be made up of anywhere between 60,000 and 100,000 troops.

A Korps was much like an army, in that it was made up of a number of *Division(en)*, or divisions, and usually also encompassed several independent units, such as reserves, training units or specialist formations. It operated below the strategic level but above the tactical level, organising the major operations of its divisions and independent units. A Korps could be made up of 40–60,000 troops.

A Division functioned at the operational level, and was usually made up of one to four *Regiment(en)*, or regiments, depending on its particular role. Sometimes a division was made up of one or two *Brigade(n)*, or brigades. In the early part of the war a typical division was made up of between 10,000 and 20,000 men. A brigade was smaller than a division, being composed of between 5,000 and 7,000 troops, distributed across several regiments. It could function, however, either independently of, or as part of a division or a Korps. A regiment operated at the tactical level, and was usually composed of between 2,000 and 6,000 troops in several *Abteilung(en)* or *Bataillon(e)* — battalions. It could also have attached to it other units, such as reserves, training units or specialist formations.

The Abteilung was a self-sufficient combat unit which operated at the tactical level. It was made up of several *Kompanie(n)*, or companies, along with any attached units, and was capable of functioning in combat without the need for assistance from other support units. To do this it had its own artillery, engineers, anti-tank crews, machine gun groups and so on. It would usually be composed of between 500 and 1,000 men.

A Kompanie operated at the tactical level, and was made up of several *Züge* (single *Zug*) or platoons. A typical Kompanie would number between 100 and 200 men, and a Zug would be made up of 30 to 40 troops. Each Zug was composed of several *Gruppe(n)*, or groups, and below this were the *Halbzug* and the *Trupp*. A Halbzug, or half platoon, was simply the name given to a unit formed when a platoon was split in two, and the Trupp, or troop, was generally made up of between 10 and 20 men.

The *Kampfgruppe(n)*, or battlegroup was an important part of the German army's modus operandi. It was a combat formation that was similar in concept to the American Task Force. It could range in size anywhere from a Kompanie (100 to 200 men) right up to a Korps (40,000–60,000 men). Most were the size of an Abteilung, and therefore composed of between 500 and 1,000 men. Kampfgruppen were often assembled to take on a specific task — such as when the *Hohenstaufen* was attacked by the Allied airborne offensive at Arnhem. There was no fixed format: they could contain artillery units, tanks, amphibious assault craft, anti-tank guns and, of course, infantry. Those at Arnhem were hastily gathered together in order to hold back the advancing British and Polish paratroopers, and were made up of whatever men and resources could be found. As with most Kampfgruppen, they were named after their leaders, and so in this instance there were Kampfgruppen called 'Harzer', 'Spindler', 'von Tettau', 'Hanke', 'Euling' and 'Frundsberg'.

Another unit used by the German army was the *Kolonne*, or column. This was an independent transportation formation of variable size used for moving equipment and supplies.

9th SS PANZER DIVISION *HOHENSTAUFEN* MAIN UNITS

19th SS Panzergrenadier Regiment
20th SS Panzergrenadier Regiment
9th SS Panzer Regiment
9th SS Artillery Regiment
9th SS Aufklärungs (reconnaissance) Abteilung
9th SS Panzerjäger (anti-tank) Abteilung
9th SS Flak (anti-aircraft) Abteilung
9th SS Pionier (engineer) Abteilung
9th SS Panzer-Nachrichten (signals) Abteilung
Divisional support units

Below: Route march by men of the SS officer training school at Bad Tölz, 1942. The school was built before the war under the eagle eye of the chief of the Waffen-SS Inspectorate, Paul Hausser. Military training ensured that the early Waffen-SS units were true elite formations. As an example, Sylvester Stadler — the final commander of *Hohenstaufen* — attended Bad Tölz where he graduated with the rank of SS-Untersturmführer.

IN ACTION

Above: Waffen-SS troops pass a knocked-out Russian JS-2 heavy tank on the Eastern Front in spring 1944. The most powerfully armed tank in the world at the time with a 122mm main gun, the JS-2 entered production in late 1943.

In December 1943, before they had even completed their training, the *Hohenstaufen* Division was assigned to I SS Panzerkorps *Leibstandarte* along with the remains of the 1st SS Panzer Division and the newly-formed 12th SS Panzergrenadier Division *Hitlerjugend*.

In early 1944 the German forces all over Europe were in a dire situation. In January, the Soviets had relieved Leningrad from German forces after a 900-day siege. On top of this the Allies were working their way up the Italian peninsula and had just landed an invasion force at Anzio. On 4 March the Soviets, under Marshal Georgi Zhukov, had launched a massive offensive on the Ukrainian front driving towards the Carpathians. This drove a large wedge into the left flank of German Armeegruppe South.

Having to fight on so many fronts at once put an enormous pressure on the army's resources, and in March 1944, as the Soviets arrived at the Polish border, the OKW moved *Hohenstaufen* into action. It was accompanied by its sister Waffen-SS division — the 10th SS-Panzer Division *Frundsberg*. Together they were incorporated into II SS Panzerkorps under the command of Paul Hausser. In this they were joined by the army's 349th Infantry and Panzer Lehr divisions.

THE EASTERN FRONT

In early March 1944, troops of the Soviet 1st Ukrainian Front mounted a major offensive aimed at positions along the Eastern Front near Skala in the Tarnopol-Proskurov sector. Their great numerical superiority meant that they were able to overpower German forces wherever they struck. Several counterattacks by the First Panzerarmee under General Hube kept them back for a while, but on 22 March five armoured corps broke through the lines followed by large numbers of infantry. They made their way south between the Zbruch and Seret rivers, and then crossed the River Dniestr. Meanwhile, other Soviet forces pushed towards them from the east in the area of Yampol and Mogilev-Podolskiy. This left the First Panzerarmee in danger of being encircled, but Hitler forbade any withdrawals or tactical repositioning. The fact that they would be completely cut off from supplies or reinforcements was, therefore, a foregone conclusion, and when the two Russian armies linked up on 25 March, no one caught in the pocket was surprised.

Although the trapped German forces had enough ammunition to survive for two weeks or more, they had very little fuel, and before long only combat vehicles were still moving. In early April 1944, II SS Panzerkorps was transported by train to the Eastern

Left: MG34 magazine change while the man at left fires a Soviet PPSh-41 SMG. The Waffen-SS used many captured Russian weapons — and there were a lot of them: by 1945 about five million PPSh-41s had been made. The circular drum magazine carried 71 rounds.

Below Left: Waffen-SS MG42 team in Russia.

Below: *Flammenwerfer* (flamethrower) 41 team prepare for action.

Above: Photograph shows the ceremony at which SS-Obersturmbannführer Otto Meyer, commanding SS Panzer Regiment 9 of *Hohenstaufen*, received his Knight's Cross on 4 June 1944. He was killed in France in September.

Below: Waffen-SS soldiers on the Eastern Front. Note that the man at back has a bayonet fixed to his rifle. The man in front is carrying wire cutters.

Front to help rescue the First Panzerarmee from its encirclement. The Soviets had issued an ultimatum that unless the German forces there surrendered immediately, they would all be shot. In order to help effect a rescue of the beleaguered troops, *Hohenstaufen* (under the XXXXVIII Armeekorps), as part of the Fourth Panzerarmee, took part in a powerful eastward counter-attack against the First Soviet Tank Army. This was launched on 5 April, with other units of the II SS Panzerkorps attacking on the flank.

The timing of this offensive was not to the Germans' advantage, however, as the arrival of spring had turned the previously frozen ground into a giant mud bath. The tanks soon bogged down and the division took massive losses. Nevertheless, the *Hohenstaufen*, fighting alongside the *Frundsberg*, kept up the pressure on the fiercely defended Soviet front.

Anecdotal evidence from a *Hohenstaufen* veteran from the 12th Company, 19th Panzergrenadier Regiment tells that during this action the Soviets attacked at Kamenets-Podolskiy in waves ten deep, where only the soldiers in the first five lines had weapons. At this stage in the war this was a common practice; after all, Stalin had more men than weapons. In order to keep their men moving forwards, the Soviets had heavily armed NKVD troops behind them — their orders were to shoot any soldiers who weren't moving quickly enough. As troops at the front fell, those behind picked up their weapons and carried on.

On 9 April, *Hohenstaufen* finally broke through Soviet lines and made contact with the 6th Panzer Division of the First Panzerarmee in Buczacz, and in doing so freed it from Russian encirclement. The next day the German front line was fully re-established.

Through the rest of April and May, *Hohenstaufen* acted as a reserve for the *Heeresgruppe Nordukraine* (Army Group North Ukraine), but while the division was refitting in preparation for a new offensive near Kovel, the Allies landed at Normandy on 6 June 1944. At first Hitler thought that Operation 'Overlord' was a feint aimed at diverting attention from the real invasion. It soon became clear, however, that this was not the case, and that massive amounts of troops and equipment had been landed successfully. This placed the Axis forces between two enormously powerful enemies. Hitler therefore cancelled plans for the II SS Panzerkorps to attack in the East,

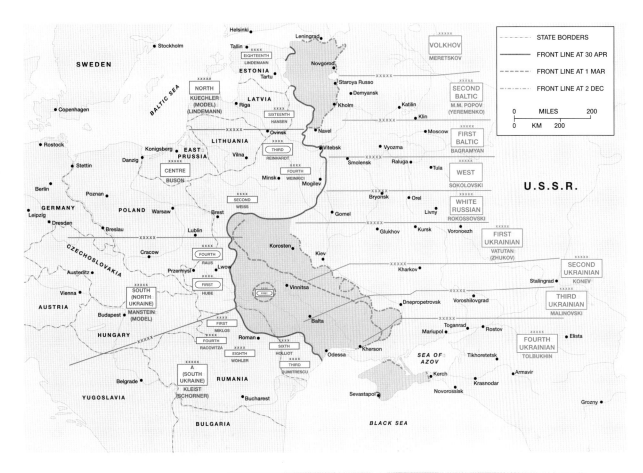

STATE BORDERS	- - - - -
FRONT LINE AT 30 APR	————
FRONT LINE AT 1 MAR	- - - -
FRONT LINE AT 2 DEC	- · - · -

Above: The Eastern Front in 1944.

Right: Waffen-SS 50mm Pak 38 anti-tank gun on the Eastern Front. Note butt and drum magazine of a Soviet PPSh-41 SMG at bottom of picture.

Above right: Waffen-SS MG42 team in the garden of a chateau near Caen.

Below right: British M4 Shermans move forward near Caen during July 1944.

and instead on 11 June ordered them to move to France under Panzergruppe West, Army Group B. The next day the first units left Poland to travel west — for most of the journey they were under continuous attack from Allied fighter-bombers.

FRANCE

Hohenstaufen reached the French border on or around 16 June, but it took several more days to reach its destination in north-western France, and another week for the rest of II Panzerkorps to arrive. The first units were unloaded from their railway carriages between Paris and Nancy on 20 June; they then moved to the south of Aunay-sur-Odan in a series of cross-country marches. At this time the division was composed of 18,000 men and 170 tanks, 21 self-propelled (SP) guns, 287 armoured halftrack personnel carriers, 16 armoured cars, 18 armoured artillery pieces and 3,670 other vehicles.

It was not the first SS Panzer division in the region, however — *Leibstandarte* and *Das Reich* were already in northern France for rest and refitting when the invasion took place. Other German forces in the area included the *Hitlerjugend* Division and the 17th SS Panzergrenadier Division *Götz von Berlichingen* under the command of Werner Ostendorff.

Hohenstaufen's mission was to help spearhead an offensive towards the beachhead. It was intended to drive a wedge between the Allied armies so that they could be encircled and defeated. The delays in reaching France caused by Allied air attacks meant, however, that by the time *Hohenstaufen* arrived, it was too late for this to work. The sheer weight of American, British, Canadian and other Allied units was more than the depleted German forces could withstand.

Before the German assault on the beachhead could be launched, however, the British pushed forward in an attempt to take Caen. This was code-named Operation

Below: Waffen-SS advance to the front during the battle for Normandy. Their SdKfz 10 halftrack is heavily camouflaged against air attack.

Above right: British armour did not fare well against the elite Waffen-SS Panzers. Here, brewed up Cromwells, Villers Bocage.

Below right: Well-known photograph of a youthful Waffen-SS MG42 gunner in France in 1944. Note the 75-round drum magazine. By the time that *Hohenstaufen* arrived in Normandy, there was a significant Waffen-SS contingent in the area. In the fighting over the next month, these forces would prove to be expert, tenacious fighters, with excellent weapons. However, Allied air superiority and its attrition of German tanks and other vehicles, gave the Allies a significant advantage.

'Charnwood'. They were met by *Hohenstaufen* at the Odon River on 28 June; this was the unit's first action on the Western Front. The next day the division fought again with British troops to the south-west of Caen as part of a counter-attack on either side of the Villers-Bocage–Noyers road. This was an attempt to assist other German troops, but it proved to be a fierce battle, and all the SS units in the area suffered severe losses; Caen itself soon fell to the Allies.

On 30 June the SS took further heavy losses when *Das Reich* and *Hohenstaufen* were attacked by the RAF who carried out a saturation raid using 250 Lancaster bombers at Villers-Bocage near Caen. The divisons were then pulled back under the cover of darkness and reassembled as a tactical reserve for II Panzerkorps in the area of Maizet-Vacognes-Montigny, with the Divisional Command Post at Le Mesnil.

On 3 July 1944, SS-Oberführer Sylvester Stadler took over command of *Hohenstaufen*. At this time its order of battle was that of a normal Panzer division, except that it did not have an anti-tank battalion (*Panzerjäger Abteilung*), as this was still being fitted out in Germany. The division was well below strength in terms of manpower and equipment, however. Most of the division was down to around 80 percent of its intended troop numbers. The Panzergrenadier regiments were even worse off: down to only 60 percent of their total expected strength — officers had been worst hit. The artillery stood at around 90 percent, the tanks at about 70 percent and other vehicles at around 80 percent. Although it was well below strength, the division was not reinforced as all available resources were channelled to other areas.

Once the Allies had established themselves near Caen west of the Orne River, they launched Operation 'Jupiter' on 10 July. This was staged by troops made up of the 43rd (Wessex) Infantry Division, along with the 46th (Highland) Brigade and a brigade of the 3rd Canadian Infantry Division. Armoured support came from the 31st Tank Brigade (7 RTR and 9 RTR) and the 4th Armoured Brigade. They had artillery support from the divisional artillery of the 43rd Wessex, the 15th Scottish, the 53rd Welsh and the 11th Armoured. They also had the heavier guns of the Second Army Group's Royal Artillery.

Operation 'Jupiter' had three objectives. The first was to stop German armoured units from withdrawing; the second was to take the high ground between the rivers Odon and Orne. The most notable feature of this area was known as 'Hill 112'. The third task was to try and secure the bridges which spanned the Orne and establish bridgeheads on the other side.

Since the Germans held Hill 112 which commanded the ground beyond the bridge over the Odon River, it was of vital importance to the Allies, and a major battle ensued for its possession. After a heavy artillery bombardment, the British VIII Corps was sent into action at dawn. They soon came up against the *Hitlerjugend, Frundsberg* and *Hohenstaufen* divisions, who were backed by the recent arrival of the *502. SS-schwere Panzer Abteilung* (2nd SS Heavy Tank Battalion). This was the Tiger battalion of II SS Panzerkorps, which had been on the road from Holland continuously for 18 days. It arrived at St Martin, about two miles south of Maltot, at 02:45 on 10 July. Their defence of the high ground was stubborn, and massive losses soon accrued on both sides. In total 15 Allied infantry battalions and six tank battalions were opposed by six German infantry battalions and five depleted Panzer battalions. Thousands of troops were killed, with the British 43rd Division losing more than 2,000 men in the first two days of fighting alone. One of the German Panzergrenadier regiments (Panzergrenadier Regiment 2) walked off the hill with only one officer and 45 men left.

On 30 July, an offensive by the British VIII Corps, code-named Operation 'Bluecoat', began at Beny-Bocage. It was intended to support the Americans by taking pressure off their left flank. By this stage of the war, Montgomery had realised that directly attacking the elite SS armoured units was futile, so in this operation he ordered his troops into

Above and Left: Two photographs showing similar scenes of fighting in Normandy, August 1944: both with knocked out Panthers. The attrition rate for German armour during the battles around Falaise was fearsome. *Hohenstaufen* would escape the pocket with fewer than 500 men and 25 tanks.

Above right: Waffen-SS man armed with a Panzerfaust inspects a knocked-out Sherman near Caen 1944.

Right: Heavily camouflaged Jagdpanzer IV in Normandy 1944. Developed as an improved version of the StuG III, over 750 were produced in 1944. Note the missing *Schürzen* — the spaced armour skirts designed to protect against shaped-charge weapons such as PIATs or bazookas.

Left: Waffen-SS soldier awaits enemy armour with his Panzerfaust. Produced initially with a range of 30m (100ft), during summer 1944 the Panzerfaust 60 doubled the range — by the end of the war it had been improved to the 150m (500ft) version.

Below: Normandy battle casualty. The tube slung around his neck carries a spare barrel for an MG34 or MG42 machine gun.

HOHENSTAUFEN OFFICIAL ORDER OF BATTLE SUMMER 1944

Division HQ
Staff
Band
9th SS (mot) Mapping Detachment
9th SS (mot) Military Police Detachment
9th SS (mot) Escort Company
1 x SP Flak Battery
1 x Motorcycle Platoon

9th SS Panzer Regiment
HQ & HQ Coy
1 x Panzer Signals Platoon
1 x Panzer Platoon
1 x Panzer Flak Battery
1 x Panzer Maintenance Company
1st Panzer Battalion
HQ and HQ Company
4 x Pz Coys (each 22 x PzKpfw V Panther)
1 x (mot) Supply Company
2nd Panzer Battalion
HQ and HQ Company
4 x Pz Coys (each 22 x PzKpfw IV)
1 x (mot) Supply Company

19th SS Panzergrenadier Regiment
HQ & HQ Company
1 x Staff Platoon
1 x Signals Platoon
1 x Motorcycle Platoon
3 x Battalions
HQ and HQ Company
1 x (mot) Supply Company
3 x (mot) Panzergrenadier Companies
1 x (mot) Heavy Panzergrenadier Company
1 x Mortar Platoon
1 x Panzerjäger Platoon
1 x SP Heavy Infantry Gun Company
1 x SP Flak Company
1 x (mot) Engineer Company

20th SS Panzergrenadier Regiment
HQ & HQ Company
1 x Staff Platoon
1 x Signals Platoon
1 x Motorcycle Platoon
1st (mot) Battalion
HQ and HQ Company
1 x (mot) Supply Company
3 x (mot) Panzergrenadier Companies
1 x (mot) Heavy Panzergrenadier Company
1 x Mortar Platoon
1 x Panzerjäger Platoon
2nd (mot) Battalion
HQ and HQ Company
1 x (mot) Supply Company
3 x (mot) Panzergrenadier Companies
1 x (mot) Heavy Panzergrenadier Company
1 x Mortar Platoon
1 x Panzerjäger Platoon
3rd (mot) Battalion
HQ and HQ Company
1 x (mot) Supply Company
3 x (halftrack) Panzergrenadier Coys
1 x (halftrack Heavy Panzergrenadier Coys
1 x Mortar Platoon
1 x Panzerjäger Platoon
1 x SP Heavy Infantry Gun Company
1 x SP Flak Company
1 x (mot) Engineer Company
HQ & HQ Pl
2 x (halftrack) Engineer Platoon
2 x (mot) Engineer Platoon

9th SS Panzerjäger Battalion
HQ & HQ Pl
2 x Jagdpanzer IV Companies
1 x (mot) Panzerjäger Conpany
1 x (mot) Supply Company

9th SS Panzer Aufklärungs Abteilung
HQ & HQ Coy
1 x Armoured Car Platoon
1 x (mot) Signals Platoon
1 x Armoured Car Company
3 (halftrack) Reconnaissance Companies
1 x Supply Company

9th SS Flak Battalion
Bn HQ & HQ Bty
3 x (mot) Heavy Batteries
1 x (mot) Medium Battery
1 x (mot) Searchlight Battery

9th SS Artillery Regiment
HQ & HQ Bty
1 x SP Flak Battery
1st SP Battalion
Bn HQ & HQ Bty
1 x SP Battery (6 x Hummel)
2 x SP Batteries (6 x Wespe)
2nd Battalion
Bn HQ & HQ Bty
2 x (mot) Batteries
3rd Battalion
Bn HQ & HQ Bty
2 x (mot) Batteries
4th Battalion
Bn HQ & HQ Bty
3 x (mot) Batteries

9th SS Engineer Battalion
Bn HQ & HQ Coy
1 x (halftrack) Recce Platoon
1 x (halftrack) Engineer Company
2 x (mot) Engineer Companies
1 x (mot) Light Panzer Bridging Train

9th SS Signals Battalion
1 x Panzer Telephone Company
1 x Panzer Radio Company
1 x (mot) Supply Column

9th SS Feldersatz Battalion
2-5 Companies

9th SS Supply Troop
HQ
6 x (mot) 120 ton Transportation Coys
1 x (mot) Supply Company
1 x (mot) Ordnance Company
3 x (mot) Maintenance Companies
1 x (mot) Maintenance Supply Column

Other
1 x (mot) Bakery Company
1 x (mot) Butcher Company
1 x (mot) Divisional Administration Platoon
2 x (mot) Medical Companies
1 x (mot) Decontamination Company
3 x Ambulances Companies
1 x Field Post Office

action against the exhausted 326th Infantry Division, which was one of the weakest units on the German front line.

The German High Command had not been expecting the British to push forward so aggressively, and they had little to hold back the advancing troops other than the natural terrain. The VIII Corps took five miles of German territory on the first day, but a counter-attack by three German Jagdpanther assault guns on the tanks of the Scots Guards destroyed 13 of their 40 Churchill tanks. Nevertheless, the Allies continued to make good ground, until they had penetrated a few miles further, when their commanders started to worry about the number of German troops behind them; as a result the advance began to run out of steam. This was not helped by the fact that some British units — particularly the Guards Armoured Division — seemed incapable of working closely with the infantry. This resulted in poor battlefield performances, and they failed to take the town of Vire before German reinforcements arrived. Had they done so, it would have been a major victory for the Allies.

On 1 August, *Hohenstaufen* was sent to deal with the threatened Allied break-through, and the division's counter-attack trapped the British 8th Rifle Brigade (3rd Infantry Division) and the 23rd Hussars (11th Armoured Division) two miles beyond Presles, south of Beny-Bocage. The Allies quickly staged a relief assault composed of the 9th and 185th Brigades (from the 3rd Infantry Division) and a combat group from the 11th Armoured Division.

Hohenstaufen was organised into several Kampfgruppen for the action, including KG 'Meyer', 'Telkamp' and 'Weiss'. An attack by KG 'Meyer' on Presles on 4 August managed to sever the British advance, but it had to relinquish the village later in the day. After three more days of heavy fighting, the Allied assault was called off.

After this *Hohenstaufen* was redeployed to the Putanges area — the move started on Sunday, 13 August, and was completed by Wednesday, 16 August. The rapidly changing battlefield situation, however, meant that the division was in a vulnerable position, and was moved almost immediately to Vimoutiers.

On the night of Thursday, 17 August, the US Third Army, along with British, Canadian and Polish forces, succeeded in surrounding the remains of 15 German divisions in an area 20 miles long by 10 miles wide. This encircled zone became known as the Falaise Pocket. Among the forces trapped there was II SS Panzer-korps, including the SS Panzer divisions *Hohenstaufen* and *Das Reich*. In all the besieged troops numbered around 100,000 men.

The Allies then proceeded to bring all their artillery and fighter-bombers to bear on the

Below: Operation 'Spring' was one of the bloodiest operations that Canadian forces took part in during the war. They suffered 18,444 casualties, including 5,021 killed. Launched on 24 July after a preliminary artillery bombardment, the Cameron Highlanders and Black Watch of Canada attacked entrenched German defenders. On 28 July *Hohenstaufen* counter-attacked and stopped the offensive in its tracks. But the British and Canadian battles around Caen did their job: they pulled in the German armour and allowed the American forces to break out to the west.

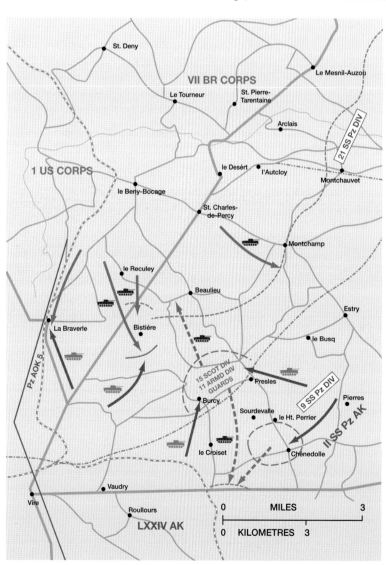

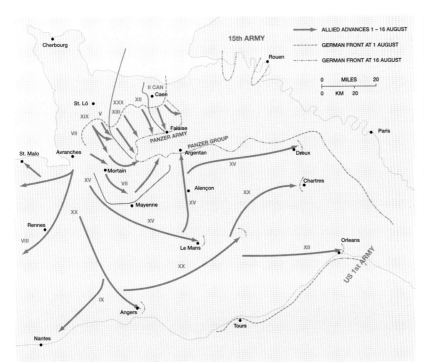

ALLIED ADVANCES 1 – 16 AUGUST
GERMAN FRONT AT 1 AUGUST
GERMAN FRONT AT 16 AUGUST

MILES 20
0 KM 20

15th ARMY

Cherbourg
Rouen
St. Lô
II CAN
XXX
XII
Caen
XIX
V
XIII
VII
Falaise
PANZER ARMY
Paris
St. Malo
Avranches
PANZER GROUP
Argentan
Dreux
XV
Mortain
XV
VII
Alençon
XV
Chartres
Rennes
Mayenne
XV
XX
VIII
XV
Le Mans
XX
Orleans
XII
US 1st ARMY
IX
Angers
Nantes
Tours

KAMPFGRUPPE 'MEYER' ORDER OF BATTLE

Attack on Presles on 4 August commanded by SS-Obersturmbannführer Otto Meyer (Oak Leaves to Knight's Cross awarded posthumously)

SS Panzer Regiment 2
Elements of SS Panzer Regiment 'H'
SS Panzer Aufklärung Abteilung 9

Left and Below: The Battle of the Falaise Gap saw the destruction of the German Seventh Armee and Fifth Panzerarmee with over 50,000 taken prisoner and wounded, and over 10,000 dead These two maps show the advance of the Allies to create the pocket and the frantic attempts by the German forces — including *Hohenstaufen* — to keep the gap from closing.

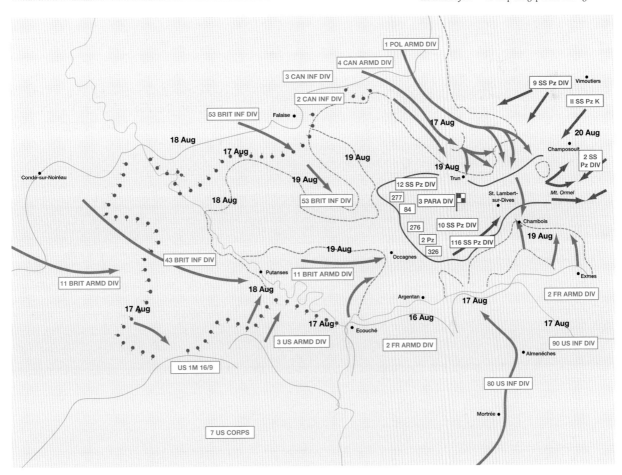

1 POL ARMD DIV
4 CAN ARMD DIV
3 CAN INF DIV
2 CAN INF DIV
9 SS Pz DIV
Vimoutiers
II SS Pz K
53 BRIT INF DIV
Falaise
17 Aug
20 Aug
18 Aug
17 Aug
19 Aug
Champosouii
2 SS Pz DIV
Condé-sur-Noiréau
19 Aug
19 Aug
Trun
12 SS Pz DIV
277
3 PARA DIV
Mt. Ormel
18 Aug
53 BRIT INF DIV
84
St. Lambert-sur-Dives
276
10 SS Pz DIV
Chambois
19 Aug
2 Pz
116 SS Pz DIV
19 Aug
326
43 BRIT INF DIV
Occagnes
11 BRIT ARMD DIV
Putanses
11 BRIT ARMD DIV
Exmes
17 Aug
18 Aug
Argentan
17 Aug
2 FR ARMD DIV
11 BRIT ARMD DIV
17 Aug
3 US ARMD DIV
17 Aug
Ecouché
16 Aug
17 Aug
90 US INF DIV
US 1M 16/9
2 FR ARMD DIV
Almenéches
80 US INF DIV
7 US CORPS
Mortrée

pocket, and massive destruction was wrought on the besieged troops. The only way out was through a small gap between Falaise and Chambois along the narrow roads beside the Dives River. The Canadians and Poles, however, tried to close this off near the settlements of Merri and Trun by attacking from the north. This resulted in some very heavy fighting, and on Friday, 18 August, the pocket had been constricted to measure just five by seven miles. By the evening the road to Trun was blocked at Mont-Ormel on the D-16. Chambois was being watched by the Americans at Bourg and by the French at Omméel and Saint-Lambert, and the Canadians were observing the bridges. There were secondary roads which led toward the slopes of Auge, Neauphe, Coudehard, Boisjos and Mont-Ormel, but this area was under the surveillance of the 1st Polish Armoured Division.

By the morning of Saturday, 19 August, the gap was almost closed, with the bridge at Saint-Lambert providing the main escape route for German troops. Almost all of their vehicles, guns and heavy weapons had to be abandoned — this was due to a severe shortage of fuel, the badly blocked roads and the incessant attacks from Allied aircraft.

Hohenstaufen, fighting alongside the 12th SS Panzer Division *Hitlerjugend*, managed to hold the Falaise Gap open for long enough for II SS Panzerkorps to escape. On 21 August 1944, they made one last assault on the gap and a few more troops managed to get through. At 16:30, however, SS-Obergruppenführer Wilhelm Bittrich ordered II SS Panzerkorps to pull back to Orbec, although it took very heavy casualties during the retreat.

Below: Allied air superiority saw fighter-bombers wreak havoc on German vehicles fleeing the Falaise Pocket.

When the Allies finally completed their encirclement at Chambois there were still around 60,000 German troops left in the pocket. At this stage the units still within the pocket included the German Seventh Armee commanded by General Hausser, the Eberbach Armoured Group, the HQ of LXXIV Korps (von Funck), LXXIVth Korps (Elfeld), XXXXVIIth Panzerkorps (Staube) and II Fallschirmkorps (Meindl). There were also remnants of several infantry divisions, including the 84th, 226th, 227th, 326th, 353rd and the 3rd Fallschirmjäger Division as well as elements of the 1st and 10th SS Panzer divisions and the 2nd and 116th Panzer divisions.

Having suffered heavy losses, II SS Panzerkorps was then pulled back across the Seine into Belgium and Holland on 22 August. During the retreat *Hohenstaufen* acted as a rearguard, and as a result had to fight for most of the way, including actions near Amiens, Orbec, Bourg-Achard, Duclair, Laon and Cambrai. Some of the fighting was so intense that it ended up as hand-to-hand combat. All this time they were also being attacked from the air by Allied fighter-bombers.

The division had performed well in northern France, in spite of losing nearly 20 percent of its original strength. SS-Oberführer Sylvester Stadler had been wounded in late July, and his temporary replacement, SS-Oberführer und Oberst der Schutzpolizei Friedrich-Wilhelm Bock was awarded Oakleaves to the Knight's Cross for his leadership during this period.

9th SS Panzer Division's Structure under Walther Harzer 29 August–10 October 1944

9th SS Panzer Regiment
19th SS Panzergrenadier Regiment
20th SS Panzergrenadier Regiment
9th SS Aufklärungs Abteilung
9th SS Artillery Regiment
9th SS Panzerjäger Abteilung
9th SS Flak Abteilung
9th SS Panzer Pionier Abteilung
Pionier Lehr Battalion 9
9th SS Panzer Nachrichten (signals) Abteilung
9th SS Sturmgeschütz Abteilung
9th SS Beobachtungs (observation) Battery
9th SS Nachschubtruppen (Supply and Logistics)
9th SS Panzer Instandsetzungs (Maintenance Unit) Abteilung
9th SS Verwaltungstruppen (Administration) Abteilung
9th SS Sanitäts (Medical) Companies
9th SS Feldlazarett (Field Hospital)
9th SS Feldgendarmerie (MP) Trupp
9th SS Ausbildungs (Training) Battalion
9th SS Wirtschafts (Logistics) Battalion
9th SS Krankenkraftwagen (ambulance) Zug
9th SS Feldpostamt (Field Post Office)
9th SS Kriegsberichter (War Correspondents) Zug
9th SS Feldersatz (Field Replacement) Battalion

Above: Waffen-SS prisoners from the Falaise Pocket.

Right: Knocked-out Flakpanzer IV *Wirbelwind* armed with a 20mm Flakvierling 38.

Above left: *Hohenstaufen* PzKpfw IV Ausf H in France during 1944.

Left: Waffen-SS grenadier.

ARNHEM

The mauling that the division had received in Northern France and then subsequently in its retreat through Belgium meant that it needed extensive reorganisation and resupply. On 3 September, the depleted *Hohenstaufen* was ordered to move to Arnhem by Generalfeldmarschall Walther Model, commander of the Sixth Panzerarmee, Armeegruppe B, for rest and a refit. They arrived in the Veluwe area, to the north of Arnhem, on 7 September 1944. Three days later, on 10 August, the division was ordered to move once again — this time back to Germany by rail for a major divisional refit. Before doing so, *Hohenstaufen* was to hand over all its weapons, vehicles and equipment, including two batteries of field howitzers, to its sister division, the 10th SS Panzer Division *Frundsberg*, which was to stay behind. At this time, the divisional strength was somewhere around 6–7,000 men. Two months earlier, the figure had been almost 16,000.

The first units were moved out on 12 September — these were mostly technical and stores personnel. On Sunday, 17 September, just before the main body of *Hohenstaufen* was due to set off on the journey back to their homeland, the skies filled with British paratroopers. At this stage there were only around 2,500 men left in the area — these were organised into 19 quick-reaction units called *Kampfgruppen* (battle groups). Named after their commanding officers, they were distributed across 12 different locations. Since the Germans had recently experienced armed uprisings from local resistance groups in other parts of Europe,

Above: Sylvester Stadler, CO of *Hohenstaufen*, was wounded in late July and replaced by SS-Oberführer und Oberst der Schutzpolizei Friedrich-Wilhelm Bock. Stadler would reach the rank of SS-Brigadeführer and become the 152nd recipient of the Swords to the Knight's Cross.

they were wary of billeting small numbers of troops in towns and cities. As a result of this the Kampfgruppen were stationed in small villages near important strategic points, such as roads and bridges.

The Second Panzerarmee was originally formed with the specific intention of defending against an Allied invasion from the Channel Coast. Consequently, many of its men had been trained to fight against airborne forces. A significant part of this training was that officers were taught to respond to the battlefield situation without waiting for orders from senior commanders. At first the massive Allied paratroop offensive took the Germans completely by surprise. They had been given no warning about it all, but their fast-response training paid off — they wasted little time in reacting and soon had an effective defence in place.

The Allied offensive, which was named Operation 'Market Garden', was intended to be a lightning-fast assault on vital bridges deep in enemy-held territory at the Dutch town of Arnhem. It was to come from two directions — an airborne assault by British paratroops from the 1st Airborne Division, and a ground attack by the British Second Army. The main objective of the high-speed attack was to give the Allies a chance to cross the Rhine before the Germans could mobilise to stop them. This would also cut off their forces in western Holland, and outflank the well-fortified Siegfried Line. If it was successful, it would leave the Allies in an excellent position to drive across the open plains

ORDER OF BATTLE DURING OPERATION 'MARKET GARDEN', SEPTEMBER 1944

German Order of Battle

Armed Forces Command Netherlands

II SS Panzerkorps
  SS-Kampfgruppe *Hohenstaufen*
  SS-Kampfgruppe *Frundsberg*

Hermann Goering Division Training Regiment
Kampfgruppe 'Von Tettau'

Army Group B

Fifteenth Armee
  LXVII Korps
    346th Infantry Division
    711th Static Division
    719th Coastal Division

  LXXXVIII Korps
    Kampfgruppe 'Chill'
    59th Infantry Division
    245th Infantry Division
    712th Static Division

1st Fallschirm Armee
  LXXXVI Korps
    176th Infantry Division
    Kampfgruppe 'Walther'
    6th Parachute Regiment
    107th Panzer Brigade
    Division 'Erdmann'

II Fallschirmkorps
XII SS Korps
  180th Infantry Division
  190th Infantry Division

363th Volksgrenadier Division (from 5 October)

Allied Order of Battle

21st Army Group

2nd British Army
  XXX Corps
    2nd Household Cavalry Regiment
    Guards Armoured Division
    43rd (Wessex) Division
    50th (Northumbrian) Division
    8th Armoured Brigade
    Royal Netherlands Brigade 'Princess Irene'

First Allied Airborne Army
  82nd Airborne Division
  101st Airborne Division

I British Airborne Corps
  1st Airborne Division
  1st Polish Independent Parachute Brigade
  52nd (Lowland) Division (airportable)

of northern Germany — an area that would be very hard to defend. It was genuinely believed that the plan could shorten the war by a year.

The paratroops were also meant to secure an 80-mile-long corridor from the Allies' front line near Eindhoven, right up to Arnhem, along which there were several bridges. The idea was that they would go in using the element of surprise, and hold the vital crossing points until ground forces could join them. A force of 10,000 paratroops was assembled, and on the morning of 17 September 1944, the operation was launched. For the previous three days, medium and heavy bombers from the US Eighth Air Force had targeted German defences along the intended air corridor. They were backed up by fighters and fighter-bombers which attacked anti-aircraft batteries, vehicles and other ground targets.

On Sunday, 17 September, at 09:45, the vast air armada of over 2,000 transport planes, gliders and tow aircraft began assembling in the skies over England. The paratroopers were packed into C-47s — these assembled into several formations, each consisting of 45 aircraft. Those troops who were not being inserted by parachute were

GERMAN ARMOUR IN THE ARNHEM AREA AT THE TIME OF 'MARKET GARDEN'

9th SS Panzer Division *Hohenstaufen*
(theatre: Arnhem–Oosterbeek–Nijmegen–Elst)
    42 x armoured cars (most halftrack)
    2 x Jagdpanzer IVs
    3 x Möbelwagen (mobile Flak full track)
    1 x Flak half track

10th SS Panzer Divison *Frundsberg* (theatre: Arnhem–Elst)
    8 x PzKpfw V Panthers
    12 x PzKpfw IVs
    4 x StuG IIIs
    7 x armoured cars, halftrack
    1 x P204 armoured scout car
    1 x Flak (vierling) halftrack

Panzer Ersatz Regiment *Bielefeld* (Panzer Kampfgruppe Mielke)
(theatre: Arnhem–Elst)
    2 x PzKpfw IVs
    6 x PzKpfw IIIs

Schwere Panzer Kompanie Hummel (theatre: Arnhem–Elst)
    12 x PzKpfw VI Tiger Is

Schwere Panzer Abteilung 506 (theatre: Oosterbeek–Elst)
    28 x PzKpfw VI Tiger IIs

Sturmgeschütz Brigade 280 (theatre: Arnhem–Oosterbeek)
    7 x StuG IIIs
    3 x StuH 42Gs

Panzer Kompanie 244 (theatre: Oosterbeek)
    1 x PzKpfw 35S
    2 x PzKpfw B2
    14 x Flammpanzer

Total number of armoured cars: 51
Total number of tanks: 104

carried by nearly 500 gliders towed by Halifax, Sterling and Albemarle bombers. A pathfinder unit was sent ahead — this was a specialist unit of paratroopers who had the task of marking out the landing and drop zones. It consisted of 12 Stirling bombers and six C-47s.

Some of the gliders broke up in mid-air as they were being towed, and as they reached the coast of mainland Europe, anti-aircraft fire also began to take its toll. The C-47 planes transporting the US 101st Airborne Division (the 'Screaming Eagles') were particularly badly hit by flak, with more than 100 of the 424 aircraft being damaged and 16 were lost. The pilots from the IX Troop Carrier Command stayed on course, however. At 12:30, the first pathfinder troops were dropped, and within half an hour they had successfully marked out the landing and drop zones.

For the German troops stationed on the ground, the first sign that the offensive was about to begin was when they heard the sound of hundreds of aircraft coming their way. As the aircraft came into view, they were shocked to see the size of the approaching air armada. One German soldier — Lt Heinz Volz from the Regiment von Hoffman — said, 'At about midday we suddenly discerned an unearthly droning noise. ... A huge stream of transport aircraft and gliders approached. ... This enormous swarm was escorted by countless fighters, in particular Lightnings [the US twin-boom Lockheed P-38 Lightning].'

At 13:00, the main body of the Allied paratroopers began dropping from the skies; at the same time the gliders were released and began their landing approaches. In the Eindhoven sector, only 53 of the 70 gliders landed safely; however, most of the 7,000 'Screaming Eagles' paratroops made it without injury. The loss of so many gliders was a serious blow, as they carried most of the 101st Airborne's heavy equipment, including anti-tank weapons, jeeps and most of their supplies.

Another 4,500 paratroopers were inserted to the east of Groesbeek Heights. These were from the 82nd Airborne Division (the 'All Americans'), some of whom landed in gliders, whereas others jumped from transport planes. At around 13:15 another 2,000

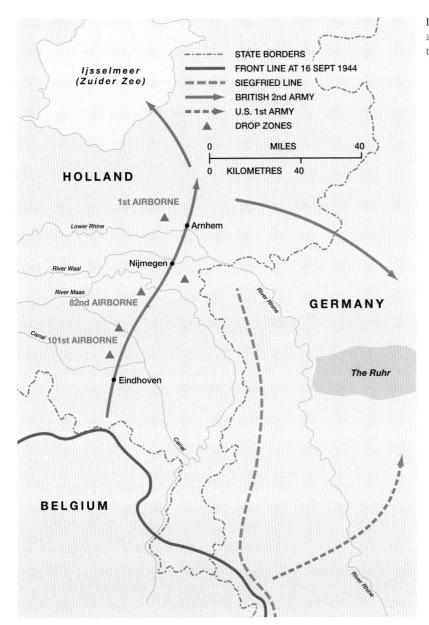

Map legend:

- STATE BORDERS
- FRONT LINE AT 16 SEPT 1944
- SIEGFRIED LINE
- BRITISH 2nd ARMY
- U.S. 1st ARMY
- ▲ DROP ZONES

0 MILES 40

0 KILOMETRES 40

Ijsselmeer (Zuider Zee)

HOLLAND

1st AIRBORNE

Lower Rhine

Arnhem

River Waal

Nijmegen

River Maas

82nd AIRBORNE

Canal 101st AIRBORNE

Eindhoven

River Rhine

GERMANY

The Ruhr

Canal

BELGIUM

River Rhine

parachuted onto a landing zone near Overasselt (east of Grave). Further troops from Company E, 2nd Battalion, 504th Regiment jumped to the west end of the Grave Bridge. The 376th Parachute Field Artillery wasted little time in getting their equipment set up, and within the hour they were providing covering fire from ten 75mm howitzers. Up to this point not many troops had landed in *Hohenstaufen*'s area, but all this changed when 300 gliders appeared above Arnhem. Although nearly 40 were shot down, the best part of 5,200 men landed safely.

When Montgomery first made his plans for Operation 'Market Garden', he did not anticipate the presence of any elite SS Panzer troops. Although the commanders of these units — the *Hohenstaufen* and *Frundsberg* divisions — were initially taken by surprise, it did not take them long to work out that the objective of the offensive was to secure the bridges leading up to and across the Rhine. These were situated at Eindhoven, Grave and Nijmegen. At 13:30, half an hour after the first Allied paratroopers began dropping,

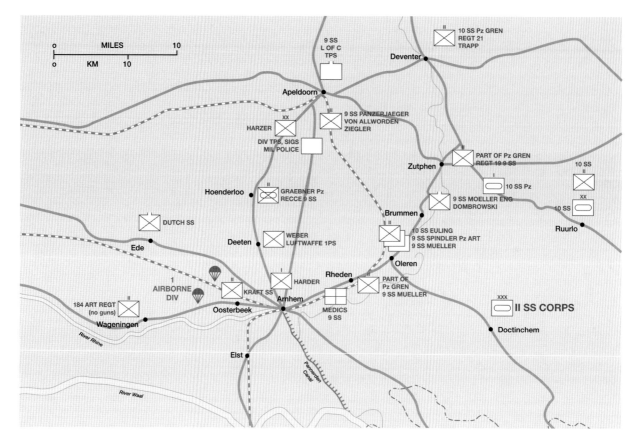

Above: The German units at Arnhem.

the commander of II SS Panzerkorps, SS-Obergruppenführer Wilhelm Bittrich, was in Doetinchem. Around this time he received the first reports of Allied paratroopers landing at Arnhem and Nijmegen, and he responded immediately by ordering the *Hohenstaufen* and *Frundsberg* divisions into defensive action.

Although many of the *Hohenstaufen*'s units had already departed, one contingent from the 16th SS Panzergrenadier Training and Reserve Battalion happened to be performing exercises in woodlands to the east of the village of Wolfheze. Although the NCOs and officers of the battalion were all veterans, the three companies — consisting of 306 men — were mostly made up of partially trained recruits. These troops, who were under the command of SS-Sturmbannführer Sepp Kraft, were coincidentally next to one of the landing zones designated for the British 1st Airborne paratroops.

As soon as the drop began, Kraft immediately set about trying to establish a defensive line to stop the Allied troops from making their way towards Arnhem. Even though he only had a small number of men with him, his plan was to delay the British for long enough to allow reinforcements to be brought up. He also sent out reconnaissance patrols and moved two companies into position — one to attack the landing zone, the other to secure the main Wageningen–Arnhem road and the Ede–Arnhem railroad. He established his battalion headquarters at the Hotel Wolfheze, and by gathering every possible man he increased the unit's troop numbers to 435.

As the British 1st Airborne landed, Kraft's men attacked them using a combination of mortar, machine gun and rifle fire. Not knowing how many British troops they were up against, Kraft was worried about being encircled, and at 18:00 he ordered his men to fall back to a stronger defensive line put together by SS-Obersturmbannführer Ludwig

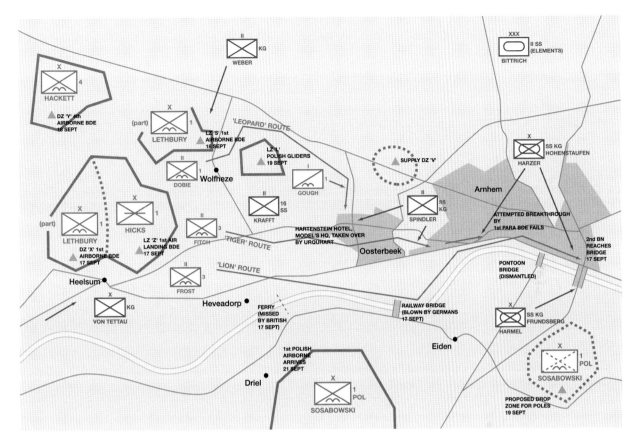

Spindler. This was being set up by the men of Kampfgruppe 'Spindler', itself composed of 16 units made up from what few troops remained in the *Hohenstaufen*'s armoured artillery regiment.

At 13:45, the Grave Bridge fell to Allied troops of the 82nd Airborne under Lt John S. Thompson. This had been one of its primary objectives, and it had been secured in less than an hour. Half an hour later, at 14:15, just before the XXX Corps began its advance, a 350-gun artillery barrage began at the Dutch-Belgian border. This, combined with bomber attacks, had the effect of decimating most of the troops who were attempting to hold the first line of German defences. Commanded by Major Helmut Kerutt, the high casualty rate left few survivors but enough survived for bitter fighting to take place. These troops managed to knock out nine Allied tanks using Panzerschrecke. For the Allies this was a major blow, as the wreckage blocked the road — the terrain on either side of the road being too boggy for other vehicles to pass by. The remaining German defenders were soon wiped out by fire from rocket-firing Typhoon fighter-bombers called in by the Irish Guards Armoured Group. They then brought up armoured bulldozers and moved the stricken tanks out of the way.

As the offensive continued, reports started filtering back to British intelligence officers about the presence of units from the Fifteenth Armee and the SS *Hohenstaufen* and *Frundsberg* Panzer divisions. They were completely stunned by this news, as they had not expected these elite forces to be between the XXX Corps and Arnhem. It was quite clear that the operation was not going to go as planned, and that at best the relief troops would be late reaching the beleaguered paratroops, if, indeed, they ever got there.

Around 15:00, British 1st Airborne troops began landing near the Tafelberg Hotel in Oosterbeek where Generalfeldmarschall Walther Model, commander of Army Group B,

Above: German attacks on British units around Arnhem.

Above: Early prisoners at Arnhem: men from Kraft's *SS-Panzergrenadier Ausbildungs and Ersatz* (Training and Reserve) *Bataillon* 16. Three British glider pilots stand at the back guarding them.

Right: Although well under-strength, *Hohenstaufen* played a major part in defeating the British. Here, SS-Grenadiers are shown with StuGs of Sturmgeschütz-Brigade 280.

Above: This photograph was taken by Luftwaffe photographer Jacobsen of PK Luftflotte 3 on 19 September. It is part of sequence of photographs that show the crucial battle as 1st Airborne's main force tried to reach Arnhem bridge. Here, the StuG IIIs of Kampfgruppe 'Möller' move into action.

Left: Captured Waffen-SS troops cut wood under guard.

had his headquarters. He was convinced that this was the Allied objective, and in a state of shock he moved to SS-Obergruppenführer Wilhelm Bittrich's II SS Panzerkorps headquarters at Doetinchem. There he formed the Kampfgruppe 'Harzer' from what remained of the *Hohenstaufen*, and sent the unit to advance on Arnhem under the command of Standartenführer Walther Harzer. These troops, who were accompanied by the 6th Parachute Regiment, had orders to reconnoitre and secure the Rhine River bridge at Arnhem. They were also to ensure that the town itself did not fall into enemy hands. The *Frundsberg* was then sent to hold Nijmegen with similar orders. Bittrich desperately wanted the bridges to be blown up so that they could not fall into Allied hands, but Model would not listen to his pleas, as he wanted them to remain standing so that he could launch his counter-attacks across them.

If matters were not already bad enough for the Allies, they got much worse when a complete set of operational plans was found by German forces in a briefcase amongst the wreckage of a crashed glider. These were handed to Generaloberst Kurt Student, who was delighted to find they listed exact details of the landing zones, objectives and timetables. As a result of this windfall, Student sent extra forces to secure the bridges targeted by the Allies.

By 15:00, the *Hohenstaufen* and *Frundsberg* divisions were beginning to take up their positions to the west of Arnhem, between the 1st Airborne and Arnhem bridge. At 15:30, lead elements of *Hohenstaufen* engaged paratroopers from the 1st Airborne in Oosterbeek, halting their advance. On top of this, the British had other problems to deal

Above: Keeping your weapon clean is a prerequisite for the infantryman. This Waffen-SS soldier is cleaning his Kar98 rifle.

Above left: The classic view of the airdrop on DZ 'X'. This aerial view of paratroops of the 1st Airborne Division airdrop was taken from a photoreconnaissance Spitfire on 17 September 1944.

Below left: Nijmegen Bridge over the Waal was captured by men of US 82nd Airborne Division and the Grenadier Guards on 20 September.

with — their radio sets had not been working properly ever since they landed. This had led to many units becoming isolated. In desperation, some of their officers tried to pinpoint each other on foot. In the confusion, several got cut off from their men, leading to further disarray.

At 18:00, just as British troops under Colonel Frost reached the bridge at Oosterbeek, the German defenders blew it up. An hour later, Hauptsturmführer Gräbner, commander of *Hohenstaufen*'s Aufklärungs Abteilung (reconnaissance battalion) crossed Arnhem road bridge at the head of a 40-vehicle column. Temporarily assigned to Armeegruppe B, his orders were to scout the roads to Nijmegen, and although his men swept both sides of the highway, they found nothing.

Less than half an hour after Gräbner's men had passed by, a small group of Royal Engineers under Captain Eric Mackay reached the 2,000ft-long Arnhem bridge. This spanned the Lower Rhine from the city on the north across to the south bank which was in open country. The British troops were then joined by others under Colonel Frost, and together they attacked the Germans defending the bridge. Frost's men had seen that a quantity of explosives was being prepared for use as demolition charges, and so they brought up a flamethrower and used it to set them off. After a fierce firefight, the Germans were beaten back — they did manage, however, to hold the south end of the bridge. The British then secured the north end, taking over some nearby buildings from where they were able to cover the bridge and the adjoining streets.

When Hauptsturmführer Paul Gräbner's *Hohenstaufen* reconnaissance battalion reached Nijmegen, they engaged the US 82nd Airborne who were approaching the bridge, pinning them down with sustained fire.

At this stage Model was still under the belief that the Allies' objective had been to capture his headquarters. Generaloberst Kurt Student, however, did his best to convince him that the operational plans that had been found in the crashed glider were genuine. Although Model was still unsure, he did make sure that information concerning further troop and supply drops were passed to all the anti-aircraft units in the area. This action proved to be of immense significance over the course of the next week, as the subsequent Allied reinforcements were severely weakened by the damage inflicted by these flak units.

Right: The StuG IIIs (three platoons) and StuH 42Gs (one platoon) of Sturmgeschütz-Brigade 280 arrrived on 19 September. This is the vehicle of the commander of the the 3rd Platoon.

Above: Waffen-SS MG34 team. The MG is mounted on its three-legged AA mount. The loader has a Kar98 slung over his back.

That evening SS-Brigadeführer Heinz Harmel, the commander of the *Frundsberg* Division, returned from Berlin after a frantic drive, arriving at about 23:30. He immediately went to see his commanding officer, SS-Obergruppenführer Wilhelm Bittrich, from whom he received an urgent briefing about the disposition of Allied forces. Bittrich ordered him to take the *Frundsberg* Division south to secure the bridge at Nijmegen. He told him at the same time that *Hohenstaufen* would deal with the British holding the north end of Arnhem Bridge.

As the first day of Operation 'Market Garden' drew to a close, the Allies were still optimistic that the situation could be salvaged, even though their intelligence concerning German troops in the area had been woefully inadequate. The US 101st and 82nd Airborne had both managed to secure their objectives, but several key bridges — especially that at Nijmegen — had still not yet been secured. Progress in establishing the land corridor from the Allied front lines to Arnhem had been very slow.

During the night of Sunday, 17 September, Kampfgruppe 'Spindler' had been working to establish a defensive line between the Ede–Arnhem road and the rail junction at Utrechtseweg. This was intended to sever the communication lines of the British units at Arnhem and to ensure that others would not be able to advance to reinforce them. By the small hours of Monday 18th, this line was in place.

Meanwhile *Hohenstaufen* had been given some extra men by the commander of the German forces in the Netherlands, General Christiansen. He had been ordered to help back up the under-strength SS units in whatever manner he could. These troops, who were under the command of Generalleutnant Hans von Tettau, the commander of

Training in Holland, were formed into Kampfgruppe 'von Tettau'. Although they were only a low-grade mix of static defence and training battalions, during the night they managed to harass the King's Own Scottish Borderers.

With the arrival of first light, von Tettau personally directed a well co-ordinated assault aimed at displacing British troops of the 1st Airborne Division from their hold on the drop zones at Wolfheze. They attacked from the west while Kampfgruppe 'Harzer' came at them from the east. Throughout this time the British radios were still not working properly, and so communications remained very poor. While only a few of von Tettau's men succeeded in taking any of the drop zones, they did succeed in stopping the British moving forward to link up with their forces at the Arnhem Bridge .

At Oosterbeek the fighting continued throughout the night, as the British attempted to reach the Arnhem Bridge, and the Germans in their turn tried to reach the Allied drop zones. Intense conflicts occurred along the front lines, although it would appear that for much of the time no one on either side actually knew where the front lines were. SS-Hauptsturmführer Möller stated that it was '... like a wild west shootout. There was no front, sections and half-sections fought scattered actions against similar size British groups. There was no discernible line on the English side either.'

At Arnhem the British paratroopers continued to arrive at the north end of the bridge, and by dawn their commander, Colonel Frost, calculated that he had around 600 or 700 men in place. Although there were several other British battalions nearby, the *Hohenstaufen* troops of Kampfgruppe 'Harzer' and the remains of the 16th SS Panzergrenadier Training and Reserve Battalion had them pinned down and as a result they were unable to reach Arnhem.

Throughout the night the British paratroops tried to take the southern end of the bridge, and twice they attempted to rush the German defences; however, both times fierce fire eventually drove them back. The Germans were no less determined to retake

Below: The battle for Arnhem Bridge — the bridge too far.

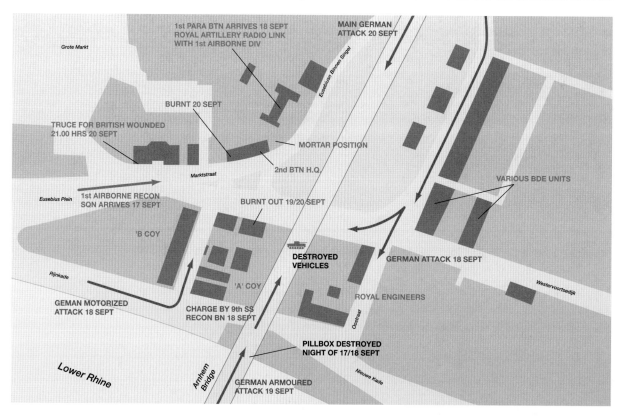

the north end of the bridge. When Hauptsturmführer Gräbner's *Hohenstaufen* reconnaissance battalion arrived in armoured vehicles, they thought that the British forces were too lightly armed to withstand a determined attack. Gräbner assessed the situation, and then set out to cross the bridge. The British lookouts saw them coming, and although their hope was that these were units of XXX Corps coming to their rescue, it was soon realised that the advancing forces were in fact Germans in armoured cars and a halftrack.

Rather than alert Gräbner's forces by opening fire too soon, the defending paratroopers waited until they were well within range. They then released a barrage from PIATs (Projectile, Infantry, Anti-Tank) and 6-pounder anti-tank guns, destroying nearly all the German reconnaissance battalion vehicles. The supporting infantry were then raked with machine-gun fire and bursts from flamethrowers. After two hours of fierce fighting, the remaining German forces withdrew to safety, although Gräbner himself — who had only been presented with the Knight's Cross by Standartenführer Harzer the day before — was killed in the action. The bridge was left covered with dead soldiers and the wreckage of burning vehicles.

The more experienced German reinforcements who were brought up to Arnhem — especially those who were veterans of the Eastern Front — expected the conflict to be only a short affair. They were shocked at the ferocity of the British defence. SS squad leader Alfred Ringsdorf, for instance, claimed that it was far worse than anything he had gone through in Russia. After some desperate actions whilst trying to clear houses, he said that: 'We fought to gain inches, cleaning out one room after the other. It was absolute hell.'

German senior commanders decided that they needed to send every available man into the action. To this end, the 3rd Battalion SS Landstorm Nederland — which at this stage was still in training in Hoogeveen — was ordered to move to Arnhem to be

Below: Arnhem bridge as seen by a photorecce Spitfire of No 16 PR Squadron on the afternoon of 18 September. That morning SS-Panzer-Aufklärungs-Abteilung 9 under SS-Hauptsturmführer Viktor Gräbner tried to pass the bridge from south to north on its way back from a recce towards Nijmegen. His SdKfz 234 armoured cars got through: the other vehicles were shot up and can be seen in the road above the bridge.

incorporated into *Hohenstaufen*. Commanded by SS-Obersturmbannführer Hermann Delfs, the unit had few weapons and only about 600 men, arranged in four companies. Since they were still untrained, Harzer decided to keep them back in reserve, but later changed his mind and added the unit to Kampfgruppe 'Spindler' to help hold the defensive line. The lack of available transport vehicles meant that SS Landstorm Nederland had to travel to Arnhem from Hoogeveen on bicycles, and it wasn't until the Monday night that they finally arrived. The next day they were moved to Betuwe to assist with the defence of Elst.

While the Germans were trying to get enough men together to mount a strong defence, the Allied advance on Eindhoven from Valkenswaard that morning had experienced many problems. Early morning fog initially prevented the tanks of the Irish Guards Armoured Group from moving forward, but when it cleared they found themselves under attack from four 88mm anti-tank guns. Under normal circumstances, this would not have been a problem as Typhoon fighter-bombers would have soon dispatched them with a rocket attack. On this occasion though, the aircraft could not fly as their bases were still fog-bound. A long delay resulted before British troops managed to silence the German gun crews by working their way around and attacking them from behind.

The Allies took another four hours to reach Eindhoven, but when they got to the Son Bridge at 19:00, it had already been blown up. Although they had made some progress, they still had another 32 miles to go to reach the besieged troops at Arnhem. Not only did they have to work out how to get across the Son River, but the US 82nd Airborne had failed to take the bridge at Nijmegen. They had, however, successfully managed to take the bridges at Grave, Heuman and Honinghutie.

At Groesbeek Heights, the landing and drop zones were coming under increasingly heavy fire from large numbers of German troops. The defending US 82nd Airborne paratroopers were outnumbered five to one, so they were not happy to hear that their

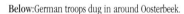

Below: German troops dug in around Oosterbeek.

Above: On 24 September PK photographer Seuffert took combat pictures around Oosterbeek. This shows one of the Sturmhaubitze 42Gs, which were armed with short-barrelled 10.5cm howitzers, of Sturmgeschütz-Brigade 280's 2nd Platoon nosing past a British parachute.

reinforcements had been delayed. Early that afternoon, another massive air armada appeared in the skies — this was composed of over 1,300 C-47s, 340 Stirling bombers and 252 B-24s escorted by around 900 fighter planes. They towed with them over 1,200 gliders, and these were packed with men and equipment vital for the operation.

The aircraft were met with intense flak as a result of the decision by Model to forewarn his anti-aircraft units of the operational plans recovered shortly after the offensive first began. These men shot down more than 20 of the escort fighters, as well as 11 bombers; they damaged a further 120.

A total of 454 gliders were designated for the US 82nd Airborne, but only 385 managed to land safely. This provided the unit with an extra 1,800 artillerymen, 177 jeeps and 60 guns. Of the 450 gliders intended for the 101st Airborne's landing zones, 428 got down safely. By this time the unit was getting short of men and ammunition, so the arrival of nearly 2,700 fresh troops along with large amounts of munitions and extra vehicles was very welcome. A lot of the supply drops ended up in German hands, however — this at a time when they were also desperate for more supplies.

As the Allied reinforcements continued to arrive, Bittrich became ever more concerned that Nijmegen Bridge might fall into enemy hands, and when Model visited him in the afternoon of Monday, 18 September, he did his best to persuade the field marshal to allow it to be blown up. Model, however, made his feelings clear — the bridge was to stay standing. In order to ensure its security, he had ordered Generaloberst Student's First Fallschirmjägerarmee to make sure the Allies were kept well to the south of this vital crossing point. He also ordered Bittrich to regain control of the bridge at Arnhem within 24 hours, so that his tanks could be pulled out of the conflict and used to stop the British advances further south. The next day — Tuesday, 19 September — the British XXX Corps reached Nijmegen.

Above: Shortly after taking the photograph on page 47, Seuffert took this photograph of infantry waiting to follow the tanks. Note NCOs with pistols and caps in front

Meanwhile at Arnhem, the British paratroopers under Colonel Frost continued to wait for reinforcements to arrive. They still held the north end of the bridge, but the fighting had been severe. The expectation was that the 1st Polish Parachute Brigade would drop on the other side of the river in the early hours of the next morning and attack the Germans from there. This would also allow them to secure the south end of the bridge.

On Wednesday, 20 September *Hohenstaufen*'s armoured reconnaissance battalion made a decisive assault on the Arnhem Bridge, and succeeded in pushing the lightly armed British paratroopers back from their positions. The same day other elements of the *Hohenstaufen* were doing their best to hold a series of strongpoints along the Waal River at Nijmegen. The Kampfgruppe 'Hanke' occupied the Fort Hof Van Holland, and the Kampfgruppe 'Euling' took over Hunner Park. At 15:00 this came under an amphibious assault launched by the 2nd Battalion, 504th Parachute Infantry Regiment of the US 82nd Airborne Division. Although Kampfgruppe 'Euling' managed to fight this attack off, they were later displaced from Fort Valkhof by the British Grenadier Guards, who then crossed the Waal between 18:00 and 19:00. Realising that Arnhem was a key factor in the offensive, the Kampfgruppe '*Frundsberg*' was then hastily withdrawn from Nijmegen to help defend the bridge there.

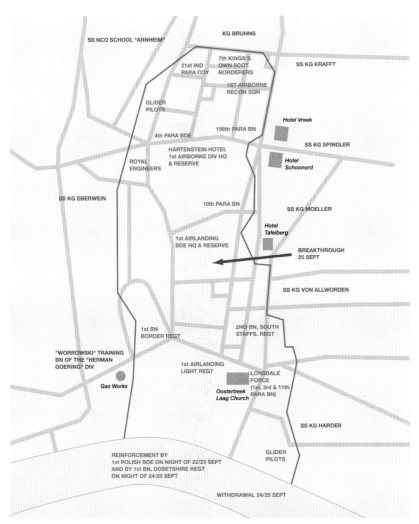

SS NCO SCHOOL "ARNHEIM"

KG BRUHNS

21st IND
PARA COY

7th KINGS'S
OWN SCOT.
BORDERERS

SS KG KRAFFT

1ST AIRBORNE
RECON SQN

GLIDER
PILOTS

Hotel Vreek

156th PARA BN

4th PARA BDE

HARTENSTEIN HOTEL
1st AIRBORNE DIV HQ
& RESERVE

SS KG SPINDLER

Hotel
Schoonord

ROYAL
ENGINEERS

SS KG EBERWEIN

10th PARA BN

SS KG MOELLER

Hotel
Tafelberg

1st AIRLANDING
BDE HQ & RESERVE

BREAKTHROUGH
25 SEPT

SS KG VON ALLWORDEN

1st BN
BORDER REGT

2ND BN, SOUTH
STAFFS. REGT

"WORROWSKI" TRAINING
BN OF THE "HERMAN
GOERING" DIV

1st AIRLANDING
LIGHT REGT

LONSDALE
FORCE
(1st, 3rd & 11th
PARA BN)

Gas Works

Oosterbeek
Laag Church

SS KG HARDER

GLIDER
PILOTS

REINFORCEMENT BY
1st POLISH BDE ON NIGHT OF 22/23 SEPT
AND BY 1st BN, DOSETSHIRE REGT
ON NIGHT OF 24/25 SEPT

WITHDRAWAL 24/25 SEPT

Left: The Oosterbeek perimeter. There was intense figting here, particularly after the remnants of the parachute troops were forced back into the perimeter. Finally, on 25 September, the defenders were given the order to leave their positions and make their way to the banks of the lower Rhine where boats awaited them. They had been brought by Operation 'Berlin' — units of 260 and 253 Field Companies, RE, and 20 and 23 Field Companies of the Canadian RE, had transported their boats from Nijmegen to Arnhem.

The next day, Thursday, 21 September, saw a determined push by *Hohenstaufen* to wipe out the British 1st Airborne Division, and they succeeded in driving them back as far as Oosterbeek. On Saturday, 23 September, the Allies were doing all they could to rescue the remaining troops of the British 1st Airborne Division. They were surrounded in Oosterbeek by the men of Kampfgruppe 'Harzer', although they were aided by the fact that the unit's heavy Tiger tanks were not suited to the town's narrow streets. Their situation was dire — they were nearly out of ammunition and, to make matters worse, further Allied supply drops that afternoon were a complete failure. All of the new equipment and ammunition was dropped on German-held territory. Meanwhile, anxious to check that all was well, SS-Obergruppenführer Wilhelm Bittrich travelled to Elst to check that everything was under control, and he was assured that the Nijmegen–Arnhem road was secure.

At Veghel, the Allied attempt to form a land corridor to Arnhem continued, albeit very slowly. British tanks and US troops from the 101st Airborne Division fought their way north against heavy opposition. At 22:00 that night, the main body of the 130th Brigade, 43rd Infantry Division, arrived at Driel.

At Arnhem, on the morning of Sunday, 24 September, Model finally received the reinforcements he had been promised ever since the Allied offensive began, when 60

newTiger tanks arrived. At this stage the besieged British forces were already on the very edge of collapsing — although they were short of manpower, their biggest problem was simply that they were almost out of ammunition. They were also experiencing regular mortar bombardments, after which there were usually attacks by armour-backed infantry. There were nearly 1,300 injured men inside the British perimeter, most of whom had been moved into the cellars of local houses. Many of the places where the wounded were lying were being hit regularly by artillery shells.

At 9:30 on the morning of Sunday, 24 September, exasperated by the conditions that the wounded men were experiencing, Dr Graeme Warrack, who was the division's chief medical officer, decided that something should be done to try and evacuate them. He sought and gained permission from his superior officer — Major General Roy Urquhart — to try and arrange a temporary truce. In order to broker the deal, Warrack walked over to the German lines under the cover of a white flag. He was quickly taken to *Hohenstaufen*'s chief medical officer, SS-Sturmbannführer Egon Skalka, who agreed that the evacuation of the large numbers of wounded men was a matter of the highest priority. Together they set out for Harzer's headquarters, where negotiations began.

Bittrich arrived shortly afterwards, and by 10:30 they had agreed that all firing would stop at 15:00 for two hours. Warrack then returned to his lines, and when the cease-fire began, did his best to help supervise the removal of the wounded of both sides by a convoy of German vehicles. At 17:00, the firing started up again, and battle was rejoined.

Elsewhere the Allies were still doing their best to drive forwards to relieve the beleaguered troops in the Arnhem area. At 18:00, Colonel Gerald Tilly, leading a part of the 43rd Infantry Division and backed by Major General Stanislaw Sosabowski's Polish paratroopers, set out from Driel and pushed towards the Rhine in an attempt to cross the river. The plan was to establish crossing points so that the entire 43rd Infantry Division could be used to try and encircle the Germans from the left flank. While these plans were being put into action, however, the commander of the trapped British 1st Airborne Division, Major General Roy Urquhart, sent a message back to Allied headquarters making it clear that his men could hold out no longer. This meant that there was insufficient time for the encirclement of German forces to take place, and so the Colonel Tilly was instead told to change his plans to help withdraw the 1st Airborne Division across the Rhine using assault craft. The boats failed to arrive on time, and in the end

Above: Tiger I Ausf E of the 3rd Company of SS Panzer Abteilung 101 in spring 1944 near Rouen. It bears the I SS Panzerkorps crossed-keys insignia and the oakleaves symbolic of the Ritterkreuz awarded to SS-Obergruppenführer Josef 'Sepp' Dietrich, whose vehicle this was. *Hohenstaufen* became part of II SS Panzerkorps in Dietrich's Sixth Panzerarmee in October 1944.

turned up several hours late in the small hours of Monday, 25 September. Although many men were successfully evacuated, large numbers were captured by the Germans before they could get away.

On Monday, 25 September, the British 43rd Wessex Division took the village of Elst, which was less than five miles from Arnhem. It was not close enough, however, and the *Hohenstaufen*'s strong defensive line proved too much for them to break through to rescue their comrades at Oosterbeek. A few Allied troops managed to escape, but after several more days of bombardment, on Friday, 29 September, the remaining British and Polish forces surrendered. They were out of ammunition and too weak to sustain their defences any longer. Of the 10,000 men who were dropped into Arnhem, only 2,300 managed to get away. 1,400 were killed in the action and over 6,000 were taken prisoner. News of the Allies' defeat was received with great joy by Hitler, who conferred the Knight's Cross of the Iron Cross on the commander of the Battle Group, SS-Standartenführer Walther Harzer.

WESTPHALIA

Before the Hohenstaufen underwent the fierce fighting at Arnhem, they were badly in need of a refit — afterwards they were in an even worse state. In early October 1944, they were moved to Bad Salzuflen, Westphalia, for rest and reorganisation as part of the

Sixth Panzerarmee under the command of SS-Oberstgruppenführer Josef 'Sepp' Dietrich. The Sixth Panzerarmee was composed of I Panzerkorps, including the *Leibstandarte* and *Hitlerjugend* divisions. The II Panzerkorps was made up of the *Das Reich, Hohenstaufen,* and Panzer Lehr divisions. SS-Obergruppenführer Wilhelm Bittrich continued to command II Panzerkorps, and SS-Oberführer Stadler commanded *Hohenstaufen.*

Hohenstaufen was divided up into various units, and these were distributed around Paderborn, Gütersloh, Siegen, Hamm and Münster. As part of the reorganisation Kampfgruppe 'Harzer' was incorporated into *Hohenstaufen* along with many extra men sourced from the Luftwaffe and various battle-scarred units. Resupplying the Sixth Panzerarmee was a slow process for two reasons — not only was the German war machine vastly over-stretched and under-resourced, but the railway system was under constant attack from the air.

While the refit was underway, the division was trained in night-fighting manoeuvres as well as how to operate with the other divisions of Sixth Panzerarmee. Throughout this period, all the units in the area had to stay camouflaged during the day to avoid attack by Allied fighter-bombers. This meant that vehicles were only able to move at night.

It was at this time that Sixth Panzerarmee was renamed Sixth SS Panzerarmee, and was commanded by SS-Oberstgruppenführer und Generaloberst der Waffen-SS Josef 'Sepp' Dietrich. The main components were *Hohenstaufen, Leibstandarte, Das Reich* and *Hitlerjugend.* Other units included the 3rd Panzergrenadier Division, the 3rd Fallschirmjäger Division and four Volksgrenadier divisions (VGDs). For political reasons, Hitler wanted to see his elite SS men outshine the regular army's forces, and so he gave them the best troops and equipment available. Sixth SS Panzerarmee was given about 500 tanks and armoured assault guns, including 90 PzKpfw VI Tiger tanks, as well as a heavy grouping of artillery.

On 12 December, Sixth SS Panzerarmee was moved to Bad Münstereifel, near Aachen, in readiness for its next operation in the Ardennes. *Hohenstaufen* was then moved to the south of Blankenheim and then shortly afterwards north to the Stadtkyll-Juenkerath-Blankenheim area.

THE ARDENNES

Hitler's last offensive on the Western Front was a push through the Ardennes. This was initially called *Unternehmen 'Herbstnebel'* (Operation 'Autumn mist'), but then renamed '*Wacht am Rhein*' (Watch on the Rhine), although it was also called the Von Rundstedt Offensive. It soon became known to the wider world, however, as the Battle of the Bulge. The German army commanders did their best to dissuade Hitler from going ahead with the plan, but he did not listen. His hope was that his forces could inflict enough of a mauling on the Allies for them to agree to a peace deal. This would avoid Germany being invaded from the west, and would allow his armies to focus on fighting back the Soviet Red Army. Hitler used all his reserve troops and what was left of the army's equipment, so it was clear that if the offensive failed, it would effectively be all over for Germany. The only issue in doubt would then be whether the Russians would get to Berlin first.

The operation was commanded by Generalfeldmarschall Walther Model, commanding Armeegruppe B. His forces were composed of the Seventh Army under General der Panzertruppen Erich Brandenberger, the Fifth Panzerarmee under General der Panzertruppen Hasso von Manteuffel and the Sixth SS Panzerarmee under Generaloberst der Waffen-SS 'Sepp' Dietrich. The Sixth SS Panzerarmee, which was the strongest of the armies taking part, was given the task of taking the bridges over the Meuse River near Liège, and then the city of Antwerp. This was the Allies' principal supply port, and so of major strategic importance.

Above: Troops of Sixth SS Panzerarmee pass a Panther. Advancing in the northern sector of the German thrust, Sixth SS Panzerarmee included I and II SS Panzerkorps. The latter was spearheaded by the 2nd SS Panzer Division *Das Reich* and by *Hohenstaufen*. *Hohenstaufen* reached its start line on 18 December and fought its way toward Manhay and Trois Ponts before being replaced by the 12th Volksgrenadiers.

Right: Fire control of a knocked out Flak 37 AA gun. The bad weather helped the German attack and ensured that Allied air superiority was nullified. As soon as the weather cleared, the paucity of German anti-air assets was revealed.

Above left: King Tiger of SS schwere (heavy) Panzer Abteilung 501 passes a line of captured US troops of 99th Infantry Division near St Vith on 18 December. The Tigers — PzKpfw VI Tiger I and II — were organized into heavy battalions and attached to larger formations. In the Ardennes there were three such units: the 501st, 506th and 301st FKL (*Funklenk* = radio-controlled). The 501st had 30 vehicles operational on 17 December — it was supposed to have 30 Tiger IIs and 45 Tiger Is. It was attached to the 1st SS Panzer Division *Leibstandarte* as part of I SS Panzerkorps.

Below left: Scavenging for supplies — German troops inspect abandoned US equiment.

Bottom left: By 22 December *Hohenstaufen* had been committed to the southern flank of *Leibstandarte*, part of I SS Panzerkorps but it was not enough. Surrounded at La Gleize, out of fuel (Luftwaffe airdrops provided enough to keep the radios running), pounded by artillery, Kampfgruppe 'Peiper' left its heavy equipment, wounded and a small rearguard, and slipped away on foot. One of the vehicles left behind was Tiger II Nr. 334 which had been blocking the American advance at Borgoumont.

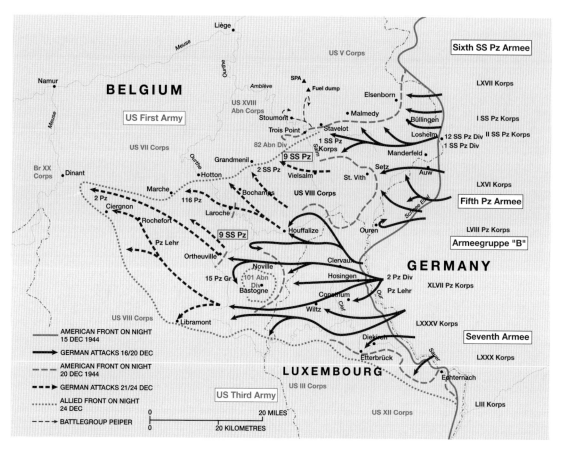

Liège

Meuse

BELGIUM

US V Corps

Sixth SS Pz Armee

LXVII Korps

Namur

Ourthe

SPA

Fuel dump

Elsenborn

US First Army

Amblève

Malmedy

I SS Pz Korps

US XVIII
Abn Corps

Stoumont

Büllingen

II SS Pz Korps

Trois Point

Stavelot

Losheim

12 SS Pz Div

US VII Corps

Meuse

82 Abn Div

1 SS Pz
Korps

Manderfeld

1 SS Pz Div

Br XX
Corps

Dinant

9 SS Pz

Grandmenil

2 SS Pz

Vielsalm

Setz

St. Vith

Auw

LXVI Korps

Hotton

Marche

Bochamps

US VIII Corps

Fifth Pz Armee

116 Pz

2 Pz

Laroche

Schnee Eifel

Ciergnon

Houffalize

Ouren

LVIII Pz Korps

Rochefort

9 SS Pz

Armeegruppe "B"

Pz Lehr

Clervaux

GERMANY

Ortheuville

Noville

15 Pz Gr

101 Abn
Div

Hosingen

2 Pz Div

Pz Lehr

XLVII Pz Korps

Bastogne

Consthum

Clef

Wiltz

Our

LXXXV Korps

US VIII Corps

Libramont

Seventh Armee

Diekirch

Etterbrück

Sauer

LXXX Korps

LUXEMBOURG

US III Corps

US Third Army

Echternach

LIII Korps

US XII Corps

AMERICAN FRONT ON NIGHT
15 DEC 1944

GERMAN ATTACKS 16/20 DEC

AMERICAN FRONT ON NIGHT
20 DEC 1944

GERMAN ATTACKS 21/24 DEC

ALLIED FRONT ON NIGHT
24 DEC

BATTLEGROUP PEIPER

0   20 MILES

0   20 KILOMETRES

The Ardennes Offensive, which began at 05:30 on 16 December 1944, started with a massive artillery barrage from just about every piece the Germans could lay their hands on. This included all manner of weapons ranging from mortars to howitzers, rocket launchers, 88mm anti-tank guns and even 14-inch railway guns. The offensive lasted from 16 December to 28 January 1945 and involved more than a million men. On the German side there were some 600,000 troops in two armies with ten corps — this was equal to 29 divisions. Facing them were around 500,000 American and 55,000 British soldiers in three armies with six corps, equalling 31 divisions.

When the opening artillery barrage ended, eight German armoured divisions and thirteen German infantry divisions struck out and attacked the troops of the five American divisions of Lieutenant General Courtney Hodges' First Army. The offensive began well, helped by a combination of surprise and bad weather. The low cloud hampered Allied air operations, making it difficult for them to fight back the combined might of the Panzer divisions. *Hohenstaufen*, fighting as part of the Sixth SS Panzerarmee headed north after breaking through the Losheim Gap alongside the Fifth Panzerarmee who then turned the other way and headed south.

The Sixth SS Panzerarmee attacked the US V Corps, which was commanded by Major General Leonard Gerow, at Elsenborn Ridge, but the Americans of the 2nd and 99th Infantry Divisions managed to hold their ground. At first the Allied commanders thought that it was a minor assault, but Eisenhower soon realised that he had completely underestimated the situation. He worked out that gaining control of the main road to the Meuse River was a critical part of the German plan, and so rushed the 101st Airborne Division to the strategically important towns of Bastogne and St Vith. The morning after they established a defensive line, the Sixth SS Panzerarmee arrived. Five days of heavy fighting then ensued, and the tide only turned in favour of the Germans when the LXVIth Corps (18th and 62nd Divisions) attacked from the east, and *Hohenstaufen* and the *Führerbegleitbrigade* came in from the north. The American troops then withdrew to regroup. Although the Germans entered St Vith on 23 December, they were too far behind schedule for the objective of taking Antwerp to succeed.

In the early stages of the offensive only parts of *Hohenstaufen* were engaged — these were the Artillery Regiment and the Reconnaissance Battalion. The rest of the division, however, was brought in after the capture of St Vith. For most of the offensive, *Hohenstaufen* fought alongside the 2nd SS Panzer Division *Das Reich*, and the Army's 560th Division under II SS Panzerkorps. To begin with, *Hohenstaufen* got further than any of the other SS divisions, but even so only reached Salmchateau, which was less than halfway to the Meuse River. The 12th SS Panzer Division *Hitlerjugend*'s advance had stalled and the 1st SS Panzer Division *Leibstandarte Adolf Hitler* had run out of fuel. Only *Das Reich* was still moving, but its movements were largely ineffective. One of the major weaknesses of Hitler's plan was that it relied on the Panzer divisions capturing American fuel dumps as they advanced. When this failed to happen, they had no reserve supplies to keep them moving.

Above: SS grenadier captured by the 82nd Airborne near Bra, five miles east of Manhay. Elements of *Das Reich* and *Hohenstaufen* were in the area at the time so he could be from either division.

Above left: Map of the German advances in the Ardennes. *Hohenstaufen* started in the north but was moved south to help take Bastogne.

Below left: German troops make their way through the heavily wooded Ardennes: these are obviously not too close to the combat!

As the defence of Bastogne drew to a close, American forces prepared for a counter-offensive — this was intended to strike out in a pincer movement to trap German units before they could withdraw from the region. The strike-back began two days before New Year, on 29 December 1944. The plan was for the US Third Army to push north, while at the same time the US First Army moved south. The intention was that they would meet at the village of Houffalize and, in doing so, would encircle a high proportion of the German forces.

On 31 December *Hohenstaufen* handed its positions over to the 12th Infantry Division and went south to help in a final desperate assault on the town of Bastogne. Despite a heavy onslaught, the American forces stood their ground, and when the weather improved a massive Allied air bombardment turned the attack into a retreat.

Hohenstaufen was then ordered to make a fresh attack using both armour and infantry near Longchamps, Belgium, on 3 January 1945. This was part of a follow-up to an operation Hitler called the 'Great Blow', which was intended to remove Allied air superiority. Most of the remaining Luftwaffe was thrown at Allied air bases in an intense bombardment. The attack did a great deal of damage, and within two hours 206 British and American planes had been destroyed. While this was indeed a blow, the Allies were able to bring up replacements, whereas their German attackers no longer had the resources to do so. The Luftwaffe's total of 300 planes and 253 pilots lost signalled that this would be its last major offensive; this meant that the Luftwaffe was no longer able to provide much in the way of air support for the beleaguered German ground troops.

Below: German armour in winter camouflage.

Left and Below: Bastogne is remembered for being the hardest nut to crack in the Battle of the Bulge. *Hohenstaufen* was pulled south after the northern thrust failed, and took part — along with 12th SS Panzer Division *Hitlerjugend* and 340th Volksdivision — in the last German offensive in the Ardennes. The attack almost took Bastogne, pushed back US 6th Armored Division but was blunted by US artillery and lack of supplies. These photographs show German prisoners marching through Bastogne on 27 December (**Left**) and a unit of US 101st Airborne Division moving east toward the enemy on 29 December.

Above: A machine gunner of the 3rd SS Panzer-grenadier Division *Totenkopf* chats to a Hungarian soldier in front of a Tiger II of 503rd schwere Panzer Abteilung. Note the tubes carrying spare machine-gun barrels slung over his shoulder. *Totenkopf* reached Budapest airport in an attempt to rescue the 45,000 troops in the city but was forced west.

The evening before *Hohenstaufen*'s attack on Longchamps took place one of the division's runners was captured by the Americans. In his possession was a case containing a full set of the attack plans. These detailed where and when the assault was to take place, and so American artillery was concentrated on the exact staging points, causing considerable damage to men and equipment. The attack went ahead despite the losses, but once again Allied airpower was too strong and the advance was slowed to a crawl. During this action *Hohenstaufen*'s 19th SS Panzergrenadier Regiment captured nearly 40 American paratroops.

By 8 January Hitler could see that both of his plans — the ground push through the Ardennes and the air offensive — were failures. Consequently, he ordered his troops to withdraw. The Allies then launched an assault on the morning of 9 January to cut the St Vith–Houffalize road — the intention being to prevent the Germans from being resupplied. As American troops moved cross-country through deep snow, they came under fire in the St Pierre–Hez forest near Bihain from tanks, artillery and anti-aircraft guns belonging to troops of the *Hohenstaufen*. A brief but fierce battle then broke out, during which time the Americans continued to advance; in doing so they flushed out and captured or killed many German soldiers. Some of these had been taking cover in foxholes covered with branches. The heavy fall of snow had covered the hideouts, and when the troops broke free they found themselves in American-held territory, and surrendered.

The Allies continued to push the German forces back, and short of fuel as well as men and equipment, Hitler ordered his troops to withdraw from the tip of the Bulge in mid-January. This decision was forced when the US First and Third Armies successfully joined up at Houffalize on 16 January. By 18 January the Americans had taken the upper hand, and the German forces were under the threat of being cut off by a northwards thrust by the US 4th Armoured Division. *Hohenstaufen* suffered heavy casualties in the Houffalize bottleneck where it tried to delay the Americans for long enough to allow other retreating German forces to escape. Before long the Allies controlled the original front prior to 16 December. On 23 January, St Vith was retaken, and on 28 January the offensive was officially over.

Overall, the Ardennes Offensive was a disaster. For a start the roads through the dense forests between Malmedy and St Vith were not suited to the passage of heavy armour. To complicate matters further, the Americans wasted little time in blowing up all the main bridges. This meant that the heavy armour had to travel further than anticipated, which resulted in major fuel shortages. Progress was far too slow for the operation to succeed, and this gave the Allies enough time to organise a robust defence. Both *Hohenstaufen* and *Das Reich* did their best to press home the attack, but under the circumstances the offensive was doomed from the start.

When the offensive ended, 81,000 US troops had been injured and 19,000 killed. The British suffered 1,400 wounded and 200 killed, and the Germans lost 100,000 killed, wounded or captured. The losses experienced by the Waffen-SS were so heavy that they were no longer officially listed as divisions, but rather as *Kampfgruppen* (battle groups). For the Allies it had been expensive in both men and materials, but at this stage in the war they had lots of newly trained soldiers and vast quantities of supplies. For the Germans, however, it was a catastrophe — they lost most of their dwindling resources, and had very little left over to defend their homeland.

HUNGARY

After the collapse of the Ardennes Offensive, *Hohenstaufen* was sent to the Kaufenheim-Mayen area for a refit. There the division enjoyed a brief spell of rest and rehabilitation, but since the Sixth SS Panzerarmee was listed as an OKW reserve, it was soon back in action. This time the division was sent east. Two SS divisions — the 8th SS Cavalry Division *Florian Geyer* and Hungarian 21st SS Cavalry Division *Maria Theresa* — had become encircled in Budapest by the Red Army, and Sixth SS Panzerarmee was needed to help them break out. They were moved to Falubattyan at the end of February, but terrible weather and poor roads prevented them from getting through to the Danube in time to be of any help to their besieged comrades. The Red Army put up stiff resistance

9th SS PANZER REGIMENT **1 February 1945**
Regt HQ and HQ Company
1 x Battalion Bn HQ 4 x PzKpfw V Panther companies
1 x Battalion Bn HQ 2 x PzKpfw IV companies 2 x Sturmgeschütz companies
Vehicles: 26 x PzKpfw IV 28 x StuG III 31 x PzKpfw V Panther 4 x Flakpanzer IV

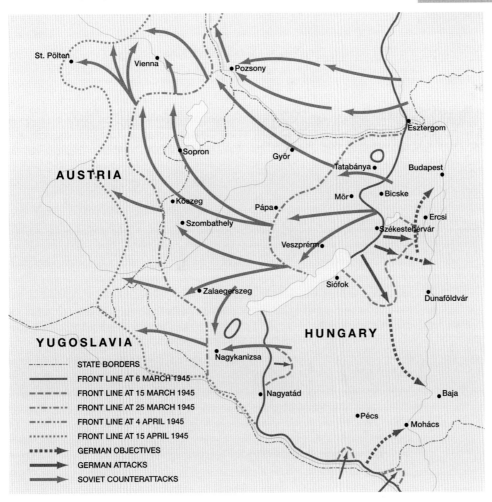

Left: The German intended (dotted red arrows) and actual (red arrows) advances in Hungary in early 1945 were halted by the Red Army who then thrust deep into the west.

St. Pölten

Vienna

Pozsony

Esztergom

Sopron

Györ

Tatabánya

Budapest

AUSTRIA

Köszeg

Pápa

Mör

Bicske

Ercsi

Szombathely

Székesfehérvár

Veszprém

Zalaegerszeg

Siófok

Dunaföldvár

YUGOSLAVIA

HUNGARY

Nagykanizsa

----- STATE BORDERS
——— FRONT LINE AT 6 MARCH 1945
- - - FRONT LINE AT 15 MARCH 1945
-·-·- FRONT LINE AT 25 MARCH 1945
-··-··- FRONT LINE AT 4 APRIL 1945
········· FRONT LINE AT 15 APRIL 1945
▶▶▶▶ GERMAN OBJECTIVES
——▶ GERMAN ATTACKS
——▶ SOVIET COUNTERATTACKS

Nagyatád

Baja

Pécs

Mohács

around the town of Sarosd, and then struck back decisively, severing the German supply lines to the north of Lake Velencei on 16 March.

All the German units in the area fared badly, but *Hohenstaufen* suffered particularly heavy losses. This forced Sixth SS Panzerarmee to retreat, but when Hitler was told he went into one of his furious tirades, claiming that the men had not tried hard enough. He ordered the 1st, 2nd, 9th and 12th divisions of the Waffen-SS to surrender their prized cuff-bands. One story has it that some men did, indeed, remove their bands. They placed them in a chamber pot, along with a severed arm, and sent the whole ensemble back to Berlin; the rest simply ignored the order.

Once again the remnants of *Hohenstaufen* fought a rearguard action, allowing many other German units to get away. Many of these battles were extremely heavy, and as they were pushed back they retreated past Jeno, Berhida, Liter, Nemesvamos, Hidekut and then to Mencseli. The Red Army then staged another offensive, driving the division back past Zalaapati, Sojtor and Paka to the *Reichsschutzstellung* (Reich protective position) — a defensive barrier on the south-east of the Reich — near Radkersburg.

AUSTRIA

The remaining components of *Hohenstaufen* had been formed into two *Kampfgruppen*, under Sixth SS Panzerarmee. After fierce battles with the Soviets they left Vienna on 13 April, and then on 26 April they were ordered to move to Amstetten to help delay the American advance. After this they were moved to the Enns-Steyr-Amstetten area on 1 May, where they surrendered to the Americans as part of the capitulation of all German forces; they marched into captivity on 8 May.

Left: Waffen-SS troops watch an SdKfz 11 halftrack towing a 75mm Pak 40.

HOHENSTAUFEN CHRONOLOGY

Period	Korps	Armee	Armeegruppe	Area
1.43–4.43	forming	-	D	Reims, Ypern
5.43–8.43	forming	15. Armee	D	Ypern
9.43–12.43	forming	-	D	Ypern
1.44–2.44	Reserve	-	D	Ypern
3.44	Reserve	19. Armee	D	South France
4.44	XXXXVIII	4. Panzerarmee	Nordukraine	Tarnopol
5.44–6.44	Reserve	4. Panzerarmee	Nordukraine	Tarnopol
7.44	II. SS	Panzergruppe West	B	Normandy
8.44	II. SS	5. Panzerarmee	B	Normandy
9.44	rebuilding	-	B	Arnhem
10.44	II. SS	1. Fallsch. Armee	B	Arnhem
11.44	rebuilding	BdE	-	Westphalia
12.44	Reserve	6. Panzerarmee	OB West	Ardennes
1.45	II. SS	6. Panzerarmee	B	Eifel
2.45–3.45	not mentioned	-	-	moving to Hungary
4.45	XXII.	2. Panzerarmee	Süd	Hungary

EQUIPMENT, MARKINGS AND CAMOUFLAGE

Above: *'Hohenstaufen'* divisional emblems — the most frequently used from the division's inception is at left; the variant at right was used in 1945.

INSIGNIA AND CAMOUFLAGE

Hohenstaufen vehicles were often identified by the H and sword insignia seen above left painted in yellow or white on AFV hulls near the driver's plate. In 1945 there were variations to this including a windmill. In combat, however, many of these identification features were camouflaged or painted out as were other identification features such as tank numbers. Vehicle insignia has been well covered in the Spearhead series — readers are recommended to read the Insignia sections in *1 21st Panzer Division* and *9 Das Reich*. Vehicle camouflage was of particular importance to *Hohenstaufen* in its fighting around the Normandy beachhead, around Falaise and in the retreat to Germany. With Allied air superiority over the battlefield, and Allied tank-busters roving the area looking for business, all Panzer movements had to be made carefully where possible under the cover of darkness or suitable camouflage — as will be seen from many of the photographs in this book; see pages 23, 42 and 50 for examples of natural camouflage.

Above: Re-enactment *Hohenstaufen* unit alongside SdKfz 251 with divisional emblem on front of vehicle.

Left: There are no obvious unit markings on this *Hohenstaufen* Panzer IV Ausf J.

Right: Waffen-SS commander of an SdKfz 251 halftrack confers with a Hauptsturmführer. Frame antennae were used on a number of 251 versions including 251/3 (*mittlerer Funkpanzerwagen* medium radio vehicle), 251/6 (*mittlerer Kommandopanzerwagen* medium command vehicle), 251/12 (*mittlerer Gerätpanzerwagen* medium artillery survey vehicle) and 251/18 (*mittlerer Beobachtungspanzerwagen* medium observation vehicle).

Below right: Waffen-SS SdKfz 251 personnel carrier with 7.92mm MG34 and armoured shield to protect the gunner as introduced on the Ausf C. Note the white paint used to provide snow camouflage.

Above: SdKfz 233 heavy, eight-wheeled armoured car. Main armament is a short-barrelled 75mm.

Left: Waffen-SS and Wehrmacht troops aboard an NSU Kettenkrad.

Left: *Hohenstaufen* Hummel on a rail car. Artillery support to panzer divisions came from such equipment as the *schwere Panzerhaubitze auf Fahrgestell PzKpfw III/IV* — a heavy armoured howitzer with a 150mm sFH18/1 L/30 gun on PzKpfw III/IV chassis.

Below left: Jagdpanzer IV/70 with a 75mm gun.

Above: SdKfz 182 Jagdpanther on the western front 1944. Armed with an 88mm Pak43/3 L/71 and a hull-mounted 7.92mm MG, the largest concentration of Jagdpanthers used in the war was in December 1944 during the Battle of the Bulge.

Below: The PzKpfw VI Tiger I was the mainstay of the heavy tank battalions. Fewer than 1,500 were built but they took a heavy toll of enemy on all fronts.

Above left: Nearly 7,750 StuG III Ausf Gs were built from December 1942.

Below left: The upgunned version of the StuG was the StuH — *Sturmhaubitze* — 42, over 1,200 of which were built before the end of the war. It was armed with an L/28 105mm howitzer.

Right: PzKpfw V Panthers being loaded onto flatcars to be shipped to the front.

Below: Crews of a Pzkpfw V Ausf A and an Sdkfz 251/6 Ausf D confer.

VEHICLES

The Waffen-SS Panzer divisions tended to get the best equipment available to German armed forces. However, *Hohenstaufen* — formed late in the war and involved in heavy fighting from the start — was often under-strength, particularly after the battle for the Falaise pocket. It can be quite difficult to be precise about actual tank strengths in any combat unit. At any one time there are vehicles in workshops, being replaced from reserve, etc. One of the best coverages of the subject is George F. Nafziger's monumental work on German orders of battle (see Bibliography). He shows *Hohenstaufen* formed with one battalion of PzKpfw V Panthers and one of PzKpfw IVs, receiving later 12 Wespe SP 105mm guns, and later still, a Sturmgeschütz Battalion. In April 1944, Hohenstaufen's Panzer Regiment had:

PzKpfw IV	StuGs	Flak 38 (t)
49	44	12

This was improved before D-Day to:

PzKpfw IV	PzKpfw V	StuGs
46	79	40

After Normandy the division was reorganized with a Panther battalion (four companies, each with 14 PzKpfw Vs) and a mixed battalion (two companies each of 14 PzKpfw IVs and two companies, each with 14 StuGs.

Above: 20mm Flak38 on an SdKfz 10/4 or 5 being used in the ground-support role. Note the gas mask containers, entrenching tools, and water bottle attached to belt.

Above left: Quadruple 20mm Flak on the Eastern Front.

Below left: Flakpanzer IV/2cm Vierling Wirbelwind.

Right: The *Hohenstaufen* cuff-title.

Below right: The commander of a Tiger I displays the characteristic black uniform of the Panzertruppen with the pink Waffenfarbe piping around his collar patches and epaulettes. The Panzergrenadier beside him is wearing two types of autumn camouflage clothing with a 'bread bag' suspended from his equipment belt. *Simon Dunstan*

Below: As the war progressed German air superiority became a thing of the past and German Panzers were increasingly masked by foliage against ground-attack aircraft known to the German troops as 'Jabos' — a contraction of *Jagdbomber*, or fighter-bomber. One crewman was usually tasked with scanning the skies for Jabos, with the dreaded Russian Shturmovik and British Typhoon being the worst culprits. *Simon Dunstan*

On 12 September 1944 the Panzerjäger (anti-tank) battalion received 28 Jagdpanzer IVs. Heavy fighting in September meant further refitting and reforming and by 2 January 1945 the division had:

PzKpfw IV	PzKpfw V	Flak Pz IV	StuGs
26	31	4	28

UNIFORMS AND EQUIPMENT

Waffen-SS uniforms and equipment have been well covered in other titles in the Spearhead series. The colour sections in *5 Leibstandarte* and *9 Das Reich* show well the camouflage combat uniforms used so extensively in Normandy and the Ardennes.

As with many of the Waffen-SS divisions, Hohenstaufen men wore a cuff-title (illustrated above right) on the left sleeve of their tunics under the SS arm eagle. They consisted of a black cloth band edged with silver braid and, as was the case with Hohenstaufen, with the unit's name on it.

The photographs that accompany this section show a variety of personal infantry weapons and anti-tank equipment—including (right) the best machine gun of the war, the MG42 7.92mm, and the excellent 75mm Panzerabwehrkanone 40 anti-tank gun. Designed by Rheinmetall Borsig, it was the standard German divisional anti-tank gun.

Hohenstaufen

Above left: The hull machine gunner/radio operator sits atop the turret of his Tiger I at the outset of an operation. The turret and hull sides of German Panzers were covered with *Zimmerit* — a corrugated paste — to prevent the attachment of magnetic anti-tank charges. *Simon Dunstan*

Left: Re-enactment scene showing Waffen-SS men in a Hanomag SdKfz 251/1 Ausf D preparing to advance with a Tiger I in support. The Panzergrenadiers in the forground display an interesting mix of Waffen-SS camouflage suits. The SdKfz 251 was the standard half-track of the Wehrmacht. Never produced in sufficient numbers to equip all units, it did reach the elite Waffen-SS formations and Panzer divisions such as *Hohenstaufen*. *Simon Dunstan*

Above: SS Panzergrenadiers march towards the front lines with their characteristic field equipment of gasmask holders, mess tins and water bottles. Their weapons include the 7.92mm Karabiner Kar98k carbine, the 9mm Solothurm SI-100 submachine gun and the Panzerfaust one-shot disposable anti-tank weapon that entered production in October 1943 at a rate of 200,000 a month.

Right: A good view of the Waffen-SS helmet runes.

Above and Below left: Anti-tank teams were essential on either front. These pictures show a typical Pak 40 on the Eastern Front.

Below: A Waffen-SS MG34 team.

Above: Waffen-SS troops fire a 50mm mortar.

Left: German machine gun team.

Above right: Waffen-SS troops. Lead man carries an MP40 SMG and the man at right an Einstossflammenwerfer 46 flamethrower.

Right: SS soldier with a 7.92mm Karabiner 98K.

Far right: The Nebelwerfer was a multi-barrelled mortar that grew in importance and numbers as the war progressed. They were organised in brigades and attached to larger units. This example is a 150mm Nebelwerfer 41.

PEOPLE

Above: SS-Obergruppenführer Wilhelm Bittrich of II. SS Panzerkorps.

SS-OBERGRUPPENFÜHRER WILHELM BITTRICH

Born: 26 February 1894 in Wernigerode
Died: 19 April 1979 in Wolfratshausen
Iron Cross 2nd Class (clasp): 25 September 1939
Iron Cross 1st Class (clasp): 7 June 1940
German Cross in Gold: 6 March 1943
Knight's Cross: 14 December 1941
With Oakleaves: 23 August 1944
With Swords: 6 May 1945

Wilhelm Bittrich was of the prewar Reichswehr clan, and as such rose to become one of the most influential characters in the Waffen-SS. He began his tenure in the SS in 1932, with the SS-Fliegerstaffel Ost, although he originally started his military career as a fighter pilot during World War I. After this he went on to command the 74 Standarte, a unit that was part of the Allgemeine-SS, until he was appointed by Himmler to be the head of the *Politische Bereitschaft* (Political Readiness Squad) on 25 August 1934. This detachment was later expanded, whereupon it became known as the Regiment 'Germania'—at this time Bittrich took over as the commander of the 2nd Company. He moved to the Regiment 'Deutschland' in October 1936, where he was the commander of the IInd Battalion. He took over as head of the 1st 'Der Führer' Regiment when it was created in early 1938, and then transferred to the *Leibstandarte* on 1 June 1939, where he served as HQ Adjutant to Sepp Dietrich. He remained there throughout the Polish campaign and then, in February 1940, he moved to the replacement section of the SS-Verfügungstruppen. On 14 December of the same year, he returned to the 2nd SS in the Regiment 'Deutschland', where he took over as regimental CO. Whilst serving in this role he was awarded the Knight's Cross, and later took over from Obergruppenführer Paul Hausser when he lost an eye in combat. Bittrich himself fell ill in January 1942 and had to step down from being divisional commander to recover. He was then transferred to become commander of the SS-Kavallerie Brigade on 1 May 1942.

He remained with the brigade until early 1943, overseeing its expansion to divisional size. He then moved on again, this time taking over command of the newly formed 9th SS Panzergrenadier Division, shortly before it was renamed *Hohenstaufen* on 19 March 1943. As with his previous unit, he supervised its expansion, building it up to full strength and ensuring that its troops were properly trained. He then took over as commander of

COMMANDERS OF THE 9th SS PANZER DIVISION *HOHENSTAUFEN*

Obergruppenführer Willi Bittrich	15 February 1943–29 June 1944
Oberführer Thomas Müller	29 June 1944–10 July 1944
Brigadeführer Sylvester Stadler	10 July 1944–31 July 1944
Oberführer Friedrich-Wilhelm Bock	31 July 1944–29 August 1944
Standartenführer Walther Harzer	29 August 1944–10 October 1944
Brigadeführer Sylvester Stadler	10 October 1944–8 May 1945

Chiefs of Staff

SS-Standartenführer Werner Ostendorff	June 1942–December 1943
SS-Standartenführer Rüdiger Pipkorn	December 1943–October 1944
SS-Obersturmbannführer Baldur Keller	October 1944–May 1945

Left: An earlier view of Bittrich as an SS-Gruppenführer.

Right: A well-known image of Sturmbannführer Sylvester Stadler in Russia, March 1943, before he became CO of *Hohenstaufen*.

the II SS Panzerkorps after Hausser left to run Seventh Army. Bittrich stayed in this position to the end of the war, and his successful defence of the Arnhem area was one of the reasons why the Allied operation 'Market Garden' failed. He was rated as one of the most chivalrous officers of the Waffen-SS.

SS-BRIGADEFÜHRER SYLVESTER STADLER

Born: 30 December 1910 in Steiermark, Austria
Died: August 1995
Iron Cross 2nd Class: 25 September 1939
Iron Cross 1st Class: 26 June 1940
Knight's Cross: 6 April 1943
With Oakleaves: 16 September 1943
With Swords: 6 May 1945

Sylvester Stadler trained as an electrician at technical school before joining the Austrian SS when he was 23. The SS transferred him to Germany for training where he later became a platoon leader in the SS-Standarte 'Deutschland'. He was sent to the officer training school at Bad Tölz in 1935 and graduated at the rank of SS-Untersturmführer. He served in the Panzer Division 'Kempf' during the Polish campaign, and then in 1940, he was transferred to the Regiment 'Der Führer' to become its company commander. On 20 September 1941 he was moved back to the 'Deutschland' where he commanded the 2nd Regiment 'Deutschland'. He was then wounded in action and sent back to Germany where he instructed at the officer training schools at Bad Tölz and Braunschweig.

By March 1942 he was considered well enough to return to front line duty, and he was assigned to the 'Der Führer', initially as commander and then as battalion commander. Whilst in this role he was awarded the Knight's Cross for his superb leadership during the winter 1941/spring 1942 battles for Kharkov. He stayed with the 'Der Führer' for some time and became regimental commander in June 1943, where he led his men throughout the battles at Kursk and the Mius River. The quality of his leadership was once again recognised and he was awarded the Oak Leaves to the Knight's Cross.

Just before he left 'Der Führer' a large number of civilians were massacred at Oradour by his men, and he asked for a court martial to clear himself from any involvement. This took place in June 1944, under Brigadeführer Lammerding, and it was found that he was not directly connected with the tragic events that took place. Indeed, the findings stated that Stadler 'enjoys great trust with his superiors, comrades and subordinates'. The same judgement also determined that he was an uncomplicated person with an open character who was neat and precise in his work, and was exemplary in both personal attitude and conduct. It went on to say that he proved to be above average in both his mental and physical abilities, that he was suitable for service in the higher army command.

He was then given command of the 9th SS Panzer Division *Hohenstaufen* in May 1944, but was seriously wounded during the fighting in Normandy. When he was fully recovered, he took over command of the division once again, rising to the rank of SS-Brigadeführer. Just before the war ended he was decorated again, this time being awarded the Swords to the Knight's Cross. During his time as a senior SS officer Stadler was recognised by his men for his bravery, and proved himself to be an outstanding leader — often doing so from the front.

SS-OBERSTURMBANNFÜHRER WALTHER HARZER

Obersturmbannführer Walther Harzer took temporary command of the 9th SS Panzer Division *Hohenstaufen* when he was only 32 on 29 August 1944. He held the post until 10 October 1944. During this period the division was in Normandy, and it got involved in some very heavy fighting. When it was trying to hold back the tanks of the US First Army at Cambrai on 2 September 1944, Harzer and his HQ became isolated from the rest of the unit when Allied armour cut through the lines. He and his men managed to escape in a convoy of vehicles under cover of darkness, and after several days of hiding from the enemy finally rejoined the division near Brussels.

The division was then moved to Arnhem to prepare for a refit. On Sunday, 17 September, just as they were due to move on to Germany, the first sounds of the massive Allied airborne assault on the area were heard. At this time Harzer was on parade in Hoenderloo. He later said that, 'As the troops were moving off to their quarters and the officers and myself were making for the officers' mess for lunch, we saw the first British parachutes in the sky over Arnhem. It could not be deduced at this stage that a large-scale operation was under way and we sat down quietly to lunch.'

As a result of the offensive, Harzer missed out on going home for his birthday celebrations, which annoyed him. Nevertheless, he did not hold this against the British when he was asked to help organise a truce to evacuate the wounded after some very heavy fighting. A British medical officer called Warrack was brought to him under the cover of a white flag, and Harzer said that, 'I spoke to Warrack who requested that the British wounded be evacuated from the perimeter since they no longer had the room or the supplies to take care of them. This meant calling a truce for a couple of hours. I agreed because ... I liked the English. I had been in England before the war as a student and had good memories of this time. I told Warrack that I was sorry that our two countries should be fighting. Why should we fight, after all? Warrack looked very haggard and worn. He was offered some cognac but refused because he said it would make him ill. He had not eaten for some time. He was given some sandwiches.'

Harzer gathered together a ragged group of railway workers, Arbeitsdienst and Luftwaffe personnel to fight the British and Polish troops, and was very proud of the way they performed. He was awarded the Knight's Cross for his superb leadership during this period; it was presented to him by Bittrich. As a person, Walther Harzer preferred the simpler things in life, and had a particular love of mechanical things. He would, for instance, rather take an engine apart than read a book.

SS-OBERSTURMBANNFÜHRER LUDWIG SPINDLER

Obersturmbannführer Ludwig Spindler became commander of the *Hohenstaufen's* Artillery Regiment at the age of 34. When he took over the unit he was a very experienced officer, having already seen a considerable amount of action. At the Battle of Arnhem he led the Kampfgruppe 'Spindler', and his leadership played an important part in the defeat of the Allied airborne troops. On the first day of the conflict, his men managed to hold a stretch of the defensive line between the railway station and the lower Rhine. In response to the size of the Allied assault force, extra troops were drafted in at short notice. This increased the Kampfgruppe's strength enough to be able to fight off the Allies' attempts to break through. He was awarded the Iron Cross and Bar, as well as the German Cross in Gold.

Above: Obersturmbannführer Walther Harzer was *Hohenstaufen's* Ia (operations officer) and was made temporary commander awaiting appointment of a new commander to replace Standartenführer Sylvester Stadler, who had been wounded in Normandy on 29 July.

Below: SS-Obersturmbannführer Ludwig Spindler.

GERMAN MEDALS AND AWARDS

Although the troops of the *Hohenstaufen* only faced combat for just over a year, they still earned their fair share of awards. The most famous medal winners were people like SS-Standartenführer Sylvester Stadler, who won the Iron Cross (1st and 2nd Class), as well as the Knight's Cross which was later supplemented by the Oakleaves to the Knight's Cross and then by the Swords to the Knight's Cross. SS-Obergruppenführer und General der Waffen-SS Wilhelm Bittrich was another recipient of the Iron Cross (1st and 2nd Class with Bar), as well as the Knight's Cross. He was also awarded the Cross of Honour 1914–1918, the 1914 Wound Badge (Black) along with the SS Honour Ring and the SS Honour Sword.

The Iron Cross
The lowest of the German medals was known as the Iron Cross, 2nd Class. This award was instituted on 1 September 1939, and was open to both men and women of any rank within the Wehrmacht, Waffen-SS or the auxiliary service organisations. This included foreign nationals who were serving as volunteers in the Wehrmacht or the auxiliary services, or if they belonged to units fighting alongside German forces. It was given for a single act of outstanding combat bravery that was deemed to be above and beyond the call of duty. As a result, it was the commonest of all the German medals, with over three million being awarded during World War II. In normal use, it was worn on a ribbon which was attached to the second button hole of the tunic. On formal dress occasions, however, it could be detached and displayed on a medal bar.

The Iron Cross, 1st Class was also instituted on 1 September 1939. In order to be eligible, candidates (who could be men or women from the Wehrmacht, Waffen-SS or the auxiliary service organisations) had to have already won the 2nd Class award. They then had to perform between three and five outstanding actions of combat bravery deemed to be above and beyond the call of duty. In all, over 450,000 were awarded during World War II. The medal itself was worn on the lower left breast of the individual's uniform.

The Knight's Cross
In all there were 12 Knight's Crosses awarded to *Hohenstaufen* soldiers. These were very highly regarded medals which were more properly known as the Knight's Cross to the Iron Cross. They were awarded either for individual heroism or for the performance of an entire unit, in which case it was given to the commanding officer. They could be won by any serving member of any branch of the Wehrmacht, Waffen-SS or the auxiliary service organisations, be they officers or men. The Knight's Cross was usually only awarded if the recipient had already won the Iron Cross 1st Class, and was given for 'outstanding actions of combat bravery above and beyond the call of duty'. During World War II there was a total of 7,361 Knight's Crosses given out; of these, 438 went to members of the Waffen-SS.

The Knight's Cross with Oakleaves
For those who had earned particular distinction, the Knight's Cross could also be awarded with various additions. The first of these was known as the Knight's Cross with Oakleaves. Like the Knight's Cross itself, it could also be given to individuals or unit commanders, including foreigners. During World War II there were a total of 890 Knight's Crosses with Oakleaves given out, of which 74 were given to the Waffen-SS.

Several members of the *Hohenstaufen* won this highly acclaimed medal, including SS-Oberführer Friedrich-Wilhelm Bock, who was presented with his award on 2 September 1944 following his outstanding leadership during the Normandy battles — especially those around the Falaise pocket, during the summer of 1944.

SS-Obersturmbannführer Otto Meyer received his award on 30 September 1944, in recognition of the quality of his leadership and for his daring on the battlefield. Other *Hohenstaufen* winners included Hauptmann Wilhelm Kohler (awarded on 4 October 1944) and SS-Obersturmbannführer Otto Paetsch (awarded on 5 April 1945).

The Knight's Cross with Oakleaves and Swords
The Knight's Cross with Oakleaves and Swords was an even higher award which was given to commanders in recognition of their unit's valour in action. Out of a total of 160 that were awarded during World War II, 24 went to members of the Waffen-SS, including that which was won by the *Hohenstaufen*'s SS-Standartenführer Sylvester Stadler.

SS-HAUPTSTURMFÜHRER KLAUS VON ALLWORDEN

SS-Hauptsturmführer Klaus von Allworden commanded the Kampfgruppe 'von Allworden' at the Battle of Arnhem. This was an infantry unit which was put together out of the remains of the dismounted tank destroyer crews of the *Hohenstaufen's* Panzerjäger Abteilung 9. At this time its strength was made up from 120 men, two SP guns and a few 75mm towed anti-tank guns. When it arrived in the area, the unit approached Arnhem from the north side. It was first active along the Dreyenseweg where it fought with the British 1 and 3 Parachute Divisions, initially ambushing and then preventing them from breaking through the defensive lines.

SS-HAUPTSTURMFÜHRER HANS MÖLLER

SS-Hauptsturmführer Hans Möller was the commander of the *Hohenstaufen's* Pionier Battalion at the time of the Battle of Arnhem. He knew the general area of operations, having fought in Arnhem and Oosterbeek in May 1940 during the invasion of the Netherlands when he was a sergeant in the SS Regiment 'Der Führer', commanding an engineer platoon. During the Allied operation 'Market Garden', his unit fought alongside the Kampfgruppe 'Gropp' for several days near the railway station just to the east of the Den Brink park. Their defensive line linked up with that of the Kampfgruppe 'Spindler', and in holding it they experienced very heavy house-to-house fighting. Under Möller's leadership the unit held out, holding back the Allied attempts to break through.

Above: SS-Hauptsturmführer Klaus von Allworden.

Below: SS-Hauptsturmführer Hans Möller.

SS-HAUPTSTURMFÜHRER PAUL GRÄBNER

SS-Hauptsturmführer Paul Gräbner was commander of the *Hohenstaufen's* Aufklärungs Abteilung (Recce Battalion). At the Battle of Arnhem he was in good spirits, having just been awarded the Knight's Cross at Hoenderloo, on 17 September by Obersturmbannführer Walther Harzer. This decoration was awarded in recognition of his leadership during the unit's armoured counter-attacks against a British breakthrough at Noyers Bocage in Normandy. At Arnhem he was ordered to cross the Rhine and look for Allied paratroopers. When he returned to the bridge, he found that the north end had been captured by the British 1st Airborne, and attempted to fight his way across. Even though he commanded the heaviest concentration of armoured vehicles in the area, he completely underestimated the strength of his opponents. As his men drove over the bridge, the British opened up with a variety of light assault weapons, destroying the vehicles and killing most of the men, including Gräbner himself.

OBERSTURMFÜHRER HERBERT ESCHER

Obersturmführer Herbert Escher commanded part of a *Funkkompanie* (radio company) in *Hohenstaufen's* signals battalion. He originally joined the SA in September 1931, and later belonged to the of the SS-Nachrichten (signals) Sturmbann. He was a signals platoon NCO in the Aufklärungs Abteilung in the *Das Reich* division when it fought in Russia until mid-December 1941. Later in the war he commanded the *Hohenstaufen's* radio company from September 1944 until the war ended in May 1945.

OBERSTURMFÜHRER GERD KNABE

Obersturmführer Gerd Knabe joined the SD in 1940 at the age of 17, when he was offered a free university education. He wanted to qualify as a lawyer, but during the welcoming speech from Gruppenführer Reinhard Heydrich, he and his fellow recruits were told that they first had to complete a tour of military duty. He took part in Operation 'Barbarossa', and was lucky to be one of the few survivors of the particularly fierce fighting that his unit — the 6th SS Gebirgs Division *Nord* — experienced on 1 July 1941, when it attacked heavily defended Soviet emplacements.

Below: The German commanders who had destroyed the British airborne side of Operation 'Market Garden' at Arnhem at the *Hohenstaufen* command post on 29 September. L-R: Generalfeldmarschall Model, Generaloberst Student, SS-Obergruppenführer Bittrich, Major Knaust and SS-Brigadeführer Harmel of the 10th SS Panzer Division *Frundsberg*. At the start of the meeting Model presented Knaust with the Knight's Cross.

Above: SS-Hauptsturmführer Paul Gräbner

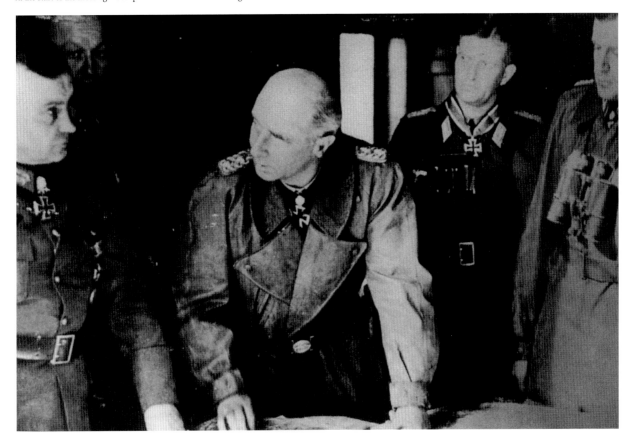

ASSESSMENT

Hohenstaufen never achieved the high profile that many of the other SS Panzer divisions established. One of the main reasons for this is that the unit did not see combat until relatively late in the war — as a result, it only existed as a fighting unit for less than a year and a half. It did, however, become known as a division that would deliver a tough fight, no matter how bad its losses were. In spite of the general perception that SS forces were barbarous killers, the *Hohenstaufen* do not appear to have had any legitimate claims made against them of this sort of behaviour. Indeed, probably the most famous episode concerning their approach to humanity occurred at Arnhem, where they agreed to a two-hour cease-fire to evacuate the wounded. They also treated the British prisoners extremely well, and so the question must be asked as to why they did not 'fit the SS mould' in this respect.

Perhaps the first issue that should be tackled is whether the SS's reputation for being bloodthirsty murderers was really justified. It is certain that many SS units were indeed guilty of consistently brutal behaviour, and as such were the perpetrators of war crimes and atrocities. It should be understood, however, that most of these were not Waffen-SS, but belonged to other elements of the SS organisation. This does not mean that all the Waffen-SS units behaved honourably: two of the most famous mass killings of prisoners were carried out by their troops. At Oradour, for instance, members of the *Das Reich* Division murdered large numbers of French civilians, and at Malmedy, soldiers from the *Hitlerjugend* executed many defenceless American prisoners.

It could be said that one reason why the troops of the *Hohenstaufen* do not appear to have participated in any war crimes is that the vast majority were only young men. While their tender age is not in question, it must be remembered, however, that most of the soldiers of the *Hitlerjugend* were also relative youngsters. The significant difference here, though, was that the ranks of the *Hohenstaufen* were mostly composed of people who had been drafted in, often against their wishes. They generally only fought out of a sense of duty to their families and their homeland and, at the end of the day, because they had no choice. On the other hand, the *Hitlerjugend* was staffed by fanatics who had been thoroughly indoctrinated from an early age.

It should not be thought, however, that the troops of the *Hohenstaufen* were anything but merciless killers on the

HOHENSTAUFEN AREAS OF OPERATIONS	
Eastern Front, southern sector	May 1943–August 1943
Italy	August 1943–October 1943
Balkans	October 1943–December 1943
France	December 1943–March 1944
Eastern Front, southern sector	March 1944–June 1944
France & Netherlands	June 1944–December 1944
Ardennes	December 1944–January 1945
Hungary & Austria	January 1945–May 1945

battlefield. There are stories that during the Battle of the Bulge German tanks were used to crush Allied soldiers in their foxholes, and in one incident a radio operator called Lawrence Silva was killed by carbon monoxide exhaust fumes when a tank was deliberately positioned over his hole and the engine revved up.

The official records compiled at the time do not indicate the true level of morale amongst the troops of the *Hohenstaufen*. Anecdotal evidence would suggest that towards the end of the war, although most of the troops fought on, there were many cases of suicides and desertions. One incidence of suicide was referred to in the regimental diary as the death of a 'mental patient'.

The troops that did fight on did so for many reasons. Some had lost all their families, friends and loved ones, and so continued out of a pathological desire to fight to the end — they were often referred to as '*Verückte Helmut*', or 'crazies'. Others knew that the brutal treatment of foreign civilians meted out by the Germans and their allies would be repaid if invading soldiers reached the German homeland, and so they fought to protect their own people.

A *Hohenstaufen* veteran — SS-Sturmmann Wolfgang Dombrowski, speaking of the battle at Arnhem — said that 'we believed the war was probably over', and yet he said that, 'Life's deeper issues did not concern us too much. We were prepared to fight on.' The Allied declaration that only an unconditional surrender would be accepted encouraged many German troops to carry on fighting as they had little to lose. A common saying at the time went, 'Enjoy the war while you can, because the peace will be terrible!' Those members of the *Hohenstaufen* who were captured before the war ended often impressed their captors with their behaviour. At Arnhem their willingness to help treat the wounded of both sides earned a lot of respect for the division.

Like all the other elite fighting units of the German Army, *Hohenstaufen* suffered massive numbers of casualties. This was largely because they were used as 'last action' forces, where only desperate fighting could save the day. In the battle for the Falaise Gap, for instance, the division was all but destroyed. One veteran, who fought in the Kampfgruppe 'Möller' at the Battle of Arnhem, remembered that afterwards there were only seven men left out of a unit that had originally been formed two years earlier from 874 soldiers. It is thought that around 250,000 SS troops were killed in World War II, and a further 400,000 were wounded. It is not known how many deserted or committed suicide.

Above: The face of battle: Waffen-SS soldier in 1945.

REFERENCE

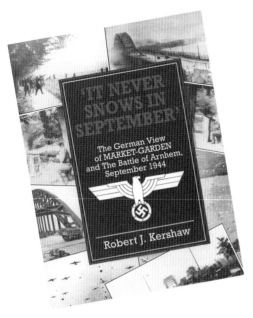

BIBLIOGRAPHY

Agte, Patrick: *Michael Wittmann and the Tiger Commanders of the* Leibstandarte; J.J. Fedorowicz Publishing, 1996.

Angolia, John R. (assisted by Stan Cook); *Cloth Insignia of the SS*, 2nd edition; R. James Bender Publishing, 1989.

Angolia, John R.: *For Führer and Fatherland: Military Awards of the Third Reich*, 3rd edition; R. James Bender Publishing, 1987.

Bando, Mark: *Breakout at Normandy: The 2nd Armoured Division in the Land of the Dead*; MBI Publishing, 1999.

Carius, Otto: *Tigers in the Mud*; J.J. Fedorowicz Publishing, 1992.

Chamberlain, Peter and Ellis, Chris; *Axis Combat Tanks*; Arco Publishing, 1977.

Davis, Brian L. and Westwell, Ian.: *Third Reich Cloth Insignia*; Ian Allan Publishing, 2003.

Duffy, Christopher: *Red Storm on the Reich: The Soviet March on Germany, 1945*; Da Capo Press, 1993.

Fey, Willi: *Armour Battles of the Waffen-SS 1943-45*; J.J. Fedorowicz Publishing, 1990.

Furbringer, Herbert: *9. SS-Division "Hohenstaufen" 1944: Normandie-Tarnopol-Arnhem*; Editions Heimdal, 1984.

Gilbert Adrian: *Waffen SS an Illustrated History*; Brompton Books. London 1989.

Kershaw, Robert J.: *'It Never Snows in September': The German View of "Market Garden" and The Battle of Arnhem, September 1944*; Ian Allan Ltd, 1994.

Kleine, Egon and Kuhn, Volkmar: *Tiger: The History of a Legendary Weapon 1942-45*; J.J. Fedorowicz Publishing, 1989.

Landwehr, Richard: *Narwa 1944: The Waffen-SS and the Battle for Europe*; Bibliophile Legion Books, 1981.

Lefevre, Eric: *Panzers in Normandy Then and Now*, 2nd edition; After the Battle, 1990.

Lumsden, Robin: *SS Regalia*; Grange Books, London 1995.

Nipe, George: *Last Victory in Russia: The SS-Panzerkorps and Manstein's Kharkov Counteroffensive February-March 1943*; Schiffer Military History, 2000.

Pallud, Jean Paul: *Battle of the Bulge Then and Now*, 2nd edition; After the Battle, 1986.

Perrett, Brian: *The Tiger Tanks*; Osprey Publishing, 1990

Reynolds, Michael: *Sons of the Reich: The History of II SS Panzer Corps*; Spellmount Publishers Ltd, 2004.

Rikmenspoel, Marc: *Soldiers of the Waffen-SS*; J.J. Fedorowicz Publishing, 1999.

Sydnor, Charles W. Jr: *Soldiers of Destruction: The SS Death's Head Division, 1933-1945*; Princeton University Press, 1990.

Tieke, Wilhelm: *The Caucasus and the Oil: The German-Soviet War in the Caucasus 1942/43*; J.J. Fedorowicz Publishing, 1995.

Tieke, Wilhelm: *In the Firestorm of the Last Years of the War, II. SS-Panzerkorps with the 9. and 10. SS-Divisions "Hohenstaufen" and "Frundsberg"*, J.J. Fedorowicz Publishing, 1999.

Walther, Herbert: *The Waffen-SS: A Pictorial Documentation*; Schiffer Military Publishing, 1990.

Winter, George: *Freineux and Lamormenil: The Ardennes*; J.J. Fedorowicz Publishing, 1994.

Yerger, Mark C.: *Waffen-SS Commanders: The Army, Corps and Divisional Leaders of a Legend: Augsberger to Kreutz*; Schiffer Military History, 1997.

INTERNET

http://www.militaria-net.co.uk/ Waffen%20SS%20Divisions.htm
This page gives a complete listing of the Waffen-SS Divisions, including the 9th SS Panzer Division *Hohenstaufen*. It shows their symbols, when they were formed and their peak troop strengths.

http://www.feldgrau.com
This is an excellent German military history research website. It focuses on the operational histories of the German armed forces between 1918 and 1945.

http://www.feldgrau.com/9ss.html
Part of the feldgrau.com website, this page focuses on the 9th SS Panzer Division *Hohenstaufen*.

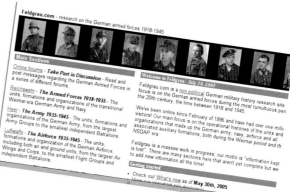

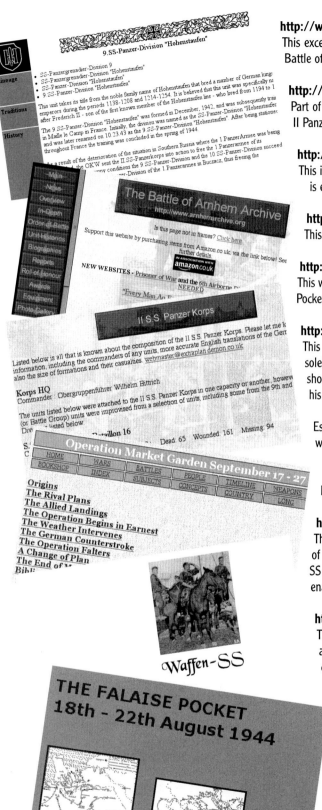

http://www.arnhemarchive.org

This excellent website presents all manner of detailed information about the Battle of Arnhem.

http://www.arnhemarchive.org/order_2SS.htm

Part of the arnhemarchive.org site, this page covers the Order of Battle of II Panzerkorps.

http://www.rickard.karoo.net/articles/battles_arnhem.html

This is another excellent website which covers the Battle of Arnhem — it is enormously detailed and well worth a visit.

http://www.axishistory.com/index.php?id=49

This website is dedicated to the history of the Third Reich and its Allies.

http://www.normandywebguide.com/falaise_pocket.htm

This website gives an excellent in-depth review of the Battle of the Falaise Pocket, and includes maps and documentary photographs.

http://www.101airborneww2.com/index.html

This website was created by World War II historian Mark Bando, who is solely responsible for its contents. Most of the photos and artefacts shown are from his personal collection and the layout and writing are his unless otherwise noted.

Especially recommended from this website is the war stories page which can be viewed at:
    http://www.101airborneww2.com/warstoriesintro.html

RE-ENACTMENT GROUP WEBSITES

http://www.geocities.com/Pentagon/Bunker/2480/

This is the website for the 9 Re-Enactment Society, which is a group of military history enthusiasts. They portray combat soldiers of the 9th SS Panzer Division *Hohenstaufen* at public displays and private re-enactments.

http://www.hohenstaufen.org/

This is the website for the 9th SS Panzer Division Historical Group, and it serves to provide information about the military traditions, customs and structure of the Waffen-SS soldier for the enthusiast and re-enactor. It also acts as an excellent reference resource for the history and the traditions of the *Hohenstaufen*.

http://9sshohenstaufen.com/frontpage.htm

This is the website for a re-enactment group which is based in the Michigan area. It portrays the *Hohenstaufen* at public educational exhibitions, lectures displays and re-enactments of typical battles fought between the Allied and Axis forces in WWII.

MUSEUMS

There is a small museum dedicated to Operation 'Bluecoat' at 14350 St. Martin-des-Besaces, Muse de la Perce du Bocage. Located in the village of Saint-Martin on N 175, about 10 km south of Caumont. Open Sundays 14:00 to 18:00 June to September. Tel : 02 31 67 52 78

MARK BANDO'S WEBSITE

TABLE OF COMPARATIVE WEHRMACHT RANKS

Army (Heer) Rank	Air Force (Luftwaffe) Rank	Waffen-SS Rank
Grenadier	Flieger	SS-Schütze
Obergrenadier		SS-Oberschütze
Gefreiter	Gefreiter	SS-Sturmmann
Obergefreiter	Obergefreiter	SS-Rottenführer
Stabsgefreiter	Hauptgefreiter	
	Stabsgefreiter	
Unteroffizier	Unteroffizier	SS-Unterscharführer
Unterfeldwebel	Unterfeldwebel	SS-Scharführer
Fähnrich		
Feldwebel	Feldwebel	SS-Oberscharführer
Oberfeldwebel	Oberfeldwebel	SS-Hauptscharführer
Hauptfeldwebel		SS-Stabsscharführer
Oberfähnrich		
Stabsfeldwebel	Stabsfeldwebel	SS-Sturmscharführer
Leutnant	Leutnant	SS-Untersturmführer
Oberleutnant	Oberleutnant	SS-Obersturmführer
Hauptmann	Hauptmann	SS-Hauptsturmführer
Major	Major	SS-Sturmbannführer
Oberstleutnant	Oberstleutnant	SS-Obersturmbannführer
Oberst	Oberst	SS-Standartenführer
		SS-Oberführer
Generalmajor	Generalmajor	SS-Brigadeführer
Generalleutnant	Generalleutnant	SS-Gruppenführer
General der	General der	SS-Obergruppenführer
Generaloberst	Generaloberst	SS-Oberstgruppenführer
Generalfeldmarschall	Generalfeldmarschall	
	Reichsmarschall	Reichsführer-SS

GROSSDEUTSCHLAND
Guderian's Eastern Front Elite
Michael Sharpe and Brian L. Davis

ORIGINS & HISTORY

Like most elite units, the *Grossdeutschland* (or *Großdeutschland* as it can be written in German) Regiment, Division and later Panzer Corps was born out of other elites, first and foremost the *Wachtruppe* (guard troop) in Berlin, and the German Army's infantry training unit based at Döberitz.

The origins of the Wachtruppe can be traced back to 1919 when groups of ex-servicemen known as the *Freikorps* had been banded together by senior German Army figures to fight the supposed threat of left wing revolution and possible invasion from Poland. An an armed body of this type was raised in Berlin and kept in being until the threat of revolution abated. This body was maintained for ceremonial duties and parades and was known as the Wachregiment Berlin until disbanded in 1921. Subsequently, as part of the army permitted to Weimar Germany, a new unit was raised under the title of Kommando der Wachtruppe (Command of the Guard Troop) and this remained unaltered for the next 13 years.

The Wachtruppe's duties were purely ceremonial. On Sundays, Tuesdays and Thursdays, with a full guard and regimental band, it would march from the barracks at Moabit, passing through the Brandenburg Gate, to rally at the Berlin war memorial. On other days simple guard changing ceremonies took place.

In 1934, after Hitler had come to power, the Kommando der Wachtruppe went through several name changes to Wachtruppe Berlin (Berlin Guard Troop) and was increased in size from seven to eight companies with a headquarters company. In 1937 the name was changed once again to Wachregiment Berlin (Berlin Guard Regiment).

The men for this unit were drawn from the newly expanded Wehrmacht, and later smaller groups were seconded to the guard regiment on half-yearly postings with NCOs being rotated yearly. These men had to be of above average height (nearly all men were six feet tall or over) and after an order was issued by Generaloberst Fritsch, had to be the best drill soldiers of their respective units. Each soldier wore a gothic 'W' on his epaulettes and received an additional 1 Groschen (a silver penny) to his daily pay for the duration of his service.

That same year, the infantry training battalion based at the Wehrmacht Infanterie-Schule at Elsgrund near Döberitz was also expanded to regimental size. This unit, which was responsible for developing many of the infantry tactics of Blitzkrieg, would contributed nearly half of its strength to *Grossdeutschland* upon its formation in 1939. From 1935 to 1939 the Infantry School was commanded by the outstanding WWI veteran Oberst Hans-Valentin Hube, who was a master of infantry tactics and wrote the standard Wehrmacht infantry training manual *Der Infanterist* (The Infantryman). German success in the early part of WWII was founded on his mobile infantry tactics, along with those practised at the Infanterie-

Lehr school in Döberitz, and those for armoured warfare developed by Heinz Guderian and Hermann Hoth at Brandenburg. These techniques, as well as parade ground drill, were practised to perfection for visiting dignitaries, heads of state and leading members of the Nazi Party.

For state visits and conferences the Wachregiment was used as a guard of honour. Their drill was perfected to very high standards and old film footage provides evidence of the precision of the parade ground training that dominated the life of the men of the Wachregiment. Long hours were spent practising arms drill and marching in formation and the unit was regularly seen on Saturday mornings parading to the sound of military marching music.

During 1938, as relations between German, and Poland, Britain and France began to deteriorate rapidly, the infantry-training regiment continued to perfect its combat techniques and the Wachregiment dutifully kept guard outside the offices wherein plans for Germany's expansion were being hatched. In the spring of 1939 German troops marched into Czechoslovakia, and Hitler's demands for territorial concessions from Poland met with rebuff. France and Britain announced their solidarity with the Poles, and in response Hitler ordered the Wehrmacht to flex its muscles. As part of this demonstration on 6 April the Wachregiment Berlin was ordered to reform as a full four-battalion infantry regiment; many of the men came from the guard troop and the others were volunteers from all across Germany.

The potential candidate had to be physically as well as mentally and morally fit (according to how these terms were understood in Nazi Germany). He had to be at least 5 feet 8 inches tall, have no criminal record and, unlike recruits for the Waffen-SS, had to have a good standard of education to serve in what was to be the premier unit of the German Army. To reflect the diversity in the ranks, the name *Grossdeutschland* (Greater Germany) was chosen for the regiment, and officially awarded to it by the town commander of Berlin, Generalleutnant Siefert, at a ceremony at the regimental barracks at Moabit on 14 June.

As Infanterie-Regiment *Grossdeutschland* (IRGD) the unit embarked on a period of reorganisation and training during the summer, training that was to prove invaluable during the Battle of France. A week before the invasion of Poland, the Führer-Begleit-Kommando (Führer Escort Command) was formed from the regiment and was then expanded to battalion strength (Führer-Begleit-Battaillon) separate from IRGD.

At the same time some 98 Wehrmacht divisions were mobilising, in preparation for the coming offensive against Poland. Throughout July and early August 1939 units moved quietly to positions east and west. On 1 September that offensive began, as 37 German divisions blitzed their way into the Polish heartland. IRGD, only recently formed, was still in the process of reorganisation and training and as such was not considered combat ready. Thus, IRGD sat out the first stage of the war. The Führer Escort Battalion, however, was involved in the 29-day campaign.

On 6 September 1939 new orders arrived stating that the IRGD was to prepare with all possible haste for an airborne attack against Poland. However, this operation was cancelled due to the advance of Soviet troops into eastern Poland, which made it unnecessary. On the 17th the unit was re-transferred to Berlin, its period of reorganisation now considered complete.

One of the companies (later expanded to a battalion) was detached and ordered to resume guard duties in the capital. On 21 October the remainder of the unit was transferred by rail to the Grafenwöhr training area south of Bayreuth, where it underwent further training and more reorganisation. By early December IRGD had been moulded into a well-disciplined and tightly controlled unit, and one that was ready for combat.

However, in Europe the fighting had met with a lull; after the surrender of Warsaw on 29 September, all German units in Poland had transferred to the west, in anticipation of an attack by Poland's allies, France and Britain. Between 6 and 11 November IRGD moved into the defensive line, taking up positions around Montbaur and Westerburg held by the XIX Motorised Army Corps, veterans of the recently concluded Polish campaign. Their commander, General der Panzertruppe Heinz Guderian was a brilliant tank leader and influential with Hitler.

Shortly after its transfer IRGD was strengthened by the arrival of two motorised assault engineer battalions,

Above: Adolf Hitler inspecting an Honour Company from Wachtruppe Berlin drawn up opposite the Reichs Chancellery in the Wilhelmstrasse, Berlin, 10 January 1936.

trained and equipped for mine-clearance, demolition and bridging. These were the 43rd Assault Engineer Battalion, with three companies, and Light Bridging Column B. Thus 1939 ended with *Grossdeutschland* having expanded from a two-battalion guard regiment to a fully trained four-battalion infantry regiment, by now under the command of Oberst Stockhausen, and actively preparing for the offensive in the west.

SPRING, 1940

During the winter lull that became known as the 'Phony War', German Army units rested and re-equipped. The Panzer units, in particular had been much reduced by the Polish campaign, and the devastatingly effective new tactics of Blitzkrieg needed further refinement.

In the last week of January, *Grossdeutschland* marched out of its Montbaur positions to new positions 100km south-west in the middle Mosel region, overlooking the Ardennes, a heavily wooded and semi-mountainous area of southern Belgium, north of the French Maginot Line, and considered impassable to tanks by British and French commanders. The regimental staff decamped to Zell, to finalise details of the upcoming campaign. The waiting dragged on and February and March passed without incident, but in early April GD gained a 16th company, Assault Gun Battery 640, whose primary weapon was the Sturmgeschütz (StuG) III, one of the early assault guns.

In the run-up to the invasion of Norway and Denmark on 9 April the regiment was put on standby alert, but again there was no counterpunch by the Allied armies, swollen to nearly 150 divisions of French (100), British (11), Belgian (22) and Dutch (10) troops. Denmark fell in a day, and although resistance in Norway continued until June, most of the country was in German control by the middle of April. *Grossdeutschland*, now under the command of Oberst Graf Schwerin, knew its time was about to come.

READY FOR WAR

Below: Before entering the *Ehrenmal*—the memorial to honour the German fallen of the Great War—to lay a wreath, Paul, Prince Regent of Yugoslavia, salutes the Honour Company from Wachregiment Berlin, 2 June 1939. On the right of the Prince Regent is the Commander of the Honour Guard and on his left is Generaloberst Fedor von Bock, Commanding Officer of Army Group 1.

By May 1940 the German Army was again ready to assume the offensive, and had 2.5 million men available for campaigning in the west. Hitler had commanded the western campaign to be fought according to a plan devised by General Manstein chief of staff to General Rundstedt, commanding Army Group A. This plan, a revision of the more conventional original plan suggested by the OKH (German Army HQ) placed great emphasis on German armoured forces and their motorised infantry, artillery and support units, and on the tactics of Blitzkrieg.

BLITZKRIEG

Late in World War I the German Army developed basic tactics that eventually evolved into modern concepts of mobile warfare. Those tactics were created in an attempt to overcome the static trench warfare of the Western Front. Elite Sturmtruppen (Stormtroop) infantry units were created to attack and break through enemy positions using the momentum of speed and surprise. However, in WWI these tactics failed to come to full fruition because of the lack of mobility and support needed in order to continue advancing deep into enemy controlled territory.

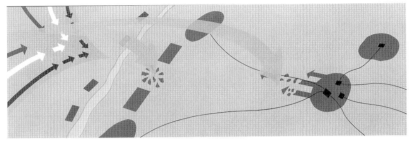

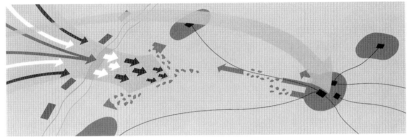

The theory of Blitzkrieg rested on the following principles:

1 Concentrated tank units break through main lines of defence and advance deeper into enemy territory, while following mechanised units pursue and engage defenders preventing them from establishing defensive positions. Infantry continues to engage enemy to misinform and keep enemy forces from withdrawing and establishing effective defence.

2 Infantry and other support units attack enemy flanks in order to link up with other groups to complete the attack and eventually encircle the enemy.

3 Mechanised groups spearhead deeper into the enemy territory outflanking the enemy positions and paralysing the rear preventing withdrawing troops and defenders from establishing effective defensive positions.

4 Main force links up with other units encircling and cutting off the enemy.

During the 1920s British military philosophers Captain Sir Basil Liddell Hart, General J.F.C. Fuller and General G. le Q.Martell further developed tactics of mobile warfare. They all postulated that tanks could not only seize ground by brute strength, but could also be the central factor in a new strategy of warfare. If moved rapidly enough, concentrations of tanks could smash through enemy lines and into the enemy's rear, destroying supplies and artillery positions and decreasing the enemy's will to resist. All of them found tanks to be an ultimate weapon able to penetrate deep into enemy territory while followed by infantry and supported by artillery and air forces.

In the late 1920s and early 1930s, Charles de Gaulle, Hans von Seekt, Heinz Guderian and many others became interested in the concept of mobile warfare and tried to implement it in the organisational structure of their respective armies.

Heinz Guderian organised Germany's tanks or Panzers into self-contained Panzer divisions working with the close support of infantry, motorised infantry, artillery and the air force. From 1933 to 1939 Germany set about mechanising a significant part of its army for the war that Hitler intended to start. In the battle for France, the motorised Infanterie-Regiment *Grossdeutschland* would play a key role.

Grossdeutschland was probably (together with the SS *Leibstandarte Adolf Hitler*) the most powerful motorised infantry unit of the German Army on 10 May 1940. Each infantry platoon had four combat squads and an anti-tank rifle. In addition to the three infantry battalions, the IRGD had a heavy weapons battalion instead of a heavy weapons company, as was normal in standard infantry regiments. This fourth battalion had one light infantry gun company (13th company) with six 75mm infantry guns, an anti-tank company (14th company) with twelve 37mm anti-tank guns, a heavy infantry gun company (15th company) with four 150mm infantry guns, one assault gun company (16th company) with six StuG III (in May 1940 the StuG III was still in its development stage and this company was one of only three German Army units equipped, for combat testing purposes, with this powerful weapon). In addition, the IRGD had received during November of the previous year a motorised assault engineer battalion, 43rd Sturm-Pionier-Abteilung, with three assault companies and one bridge company.

On the eve of the attack, GD was at its start point in the Mosel, and ready for battle.

Left: Small-bore gunnery training at one of the artillery schools.

Opposite page, above: Troops from Wachtruppe Berlin parade for the Commander-in-Chief of the German Army, General der Artillerie Freiherr von Fritsch, Moabit parade ground, Berlin, 5 December 1935.

Opposite page, below: Parade for the Royal Belgian Special Commission to Berlin. Following a wreath-laying ceremony , the Fife and Drum Corps from the Honour Company of Wachtruppe Berlin parade down Unter den Linden, past the *Ehrenmal*, Berlin.

Below: A Guard of Honour from Infantry Regiment *Grossdeutschland* drawn up in front of Anhalter main line railway station, Berlin, present arms for review by the Soviet Foreign Minister Vyacheslav Molotov, the Chairman of the Soviet of People's Commissars of the USSR, prior to his departure for Russia, 12 November 1940. Molotov is seen here accompanied by Field Marshal Wilhelm Keitel (far left), and the German Foreign Minister, Joachim von Ribbentrop.

**INFANTRY REGIMENT (MOT) *GROSSDEUTSCHLAND*
as at 10 May 1940**

RHQ

Infantry Battalion (mot) I

Bn HQ
- 2 x Lt Telephone Sect
- 4 x Pack Radio Sect
- 2 x Pack Radio Sect

- 3 x Infantry Coys
  Coy HQ and HQ Sect
  - 3 x Inf Platoons
    - HQ Section
    - 4 x Infantry Squads
    - 1 x Mortar Section

- 1 x MG Coy (Mot)
  Coy HQ
  - 3 x MG Platoons
    - HQ Section
    - 2 x MG Sections

- 1 x Mortar Pl
  - HQ Section
  - 3 x Mortar Sections

Signal Platoon (mot)

Platoon HQ
- 4 x Lt Telephone Sects
- 4 x Lt Radio Sects
- 6 x Pack Radio Sects

**640th Assault Gun
(Sturmgeschütz) Battery**

Battery HQ
- 3 x Assault Gun Platoons
  - Each of HQ Sect,
    Ammo Sect, Gun Sect
    (2 x Sd Kfz 142)

1 MC Messenger Pl

Platoon HQ
- 5 x Sections

Infantry Battalion (mot) II

Bn HQ
- 2 x Lt Telephone Sect
- 4 x Pack Radio Sect
- 2 x Pack Radio Sect

- 3 x Infantry Coys
  Coy HQ and HQ Sect
  - 3 x Inf Platoons
    - HQ Section
    - 4 x Infantry Squads
    - 1 x Mortar Section

- 1 x MG Coy (Mot)
  Coy HQ
  - 3 x MG Platoons
    - HQ Section
    - 2 x MG Sections

- 1 x Mortar Pl
  - HQ Section
  - 3 x Mortar Sections

Infantry Battalion (mot) III

Bn HQ
- 2 x Lt Telephone Sect
- 4 x Pack Radio Sect
- 2 x Pack Radio Sect

- 3 x Infantry Coys
  Coy HQ and HQ Sect
  - 3 x Inf Platoons
    - HQ Section
    - 4 x Infantry Squads
    - 1 x Mortar Section

- 1 x MG Coy (Mot)
  Coy HQ
  - 3 x MG Platoons
    - HQ Section
    - 2 x MG Sections

- 1 x Mortar Pl
  - HQ Section
  - 3 x Mortar Sections

Infantry Battalion (mot) IV

Bn HQ
- 2 x Lt Telephone Sect
- 4 x Pack Radio Sect
- 2 x Pack Radio Sect

- Lt Inf Gun Coy (mot)
  Coy HQ with HQ Sect and
      Lt Telephone Sect
  - 3 x Lt Inf Gun Platoons
    - HQ Section
    - 1 x Lt Telephone Sect
    - 1 x Ammo Sect
    - 1 x Gun Sect (2 x 75mm)

- 1 x PzJg Coy (Mot)
  Coy HQ
  4 x PzJg Platoons
    - HQ Section
    - 2 x MG Sections

- 1 x Hy Inf Gun Coy (Mot)
  Coy HQ
    - HQ Section
    - 2 x Lt Telephone Sections
    - 2 x Pack Radio Sections
  - 2 x Hy Inf Gun Platoons
    - HQ Section
    - 1 x Lt Telephone Section
    - 1 x Ammo Section
    - 1 x Gun Section
      (2 x 150mm)

Above right: A camouflaged anti-tank gun, a 50mm Pak (*Panzerabwehrkanone*) 38, manned by troops of Infantry Regiment Grossdeutschland, supporting a assault somewhere on the Eastern Front.

Right: German infantry prepare to jump-off. They are wearing backpacks and carrying support weaponry; the man second from left is carrying a 5cm light mortar.

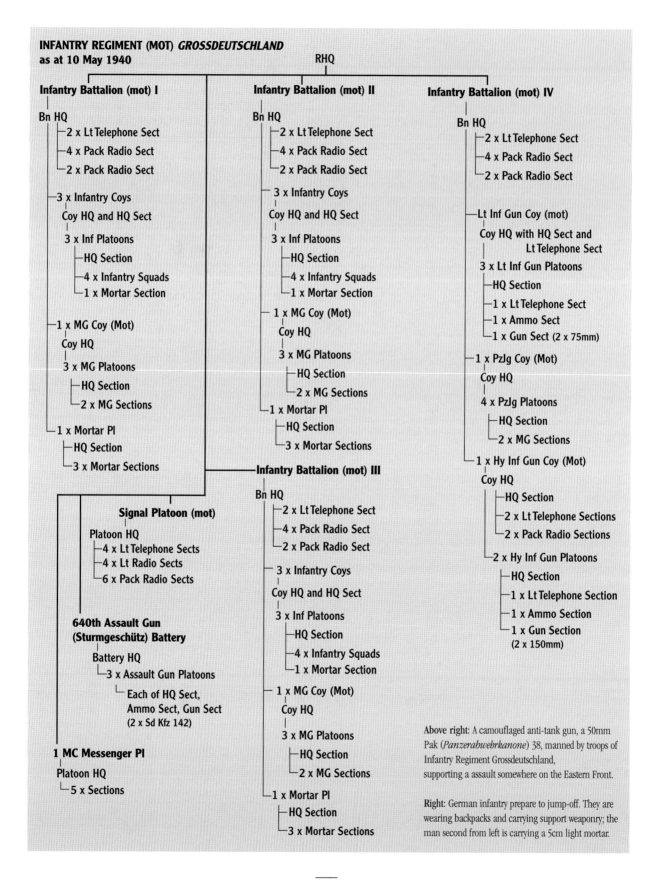

IN ACTION

Above right: An MG 34 heavy-machine gun and crew covering a length of tree-lined country road.

Below right: The German invasion of the west in 1940. *Grossdeutschland* was part of Guderian's XIX Corps in the offensive.

1940: THE WESTERN OFFENSIVE

For the offensive, three army groups, A, B and C, under Rundstedt, Bock and Leeb respectively, were created. The key tank units, including the 5th and 7th Panzers of Hoth's group, the Kleist Armoured Group (with the XIX Corps under Guderian) and the 6th and 8th Panzers under Reinhardt, were attached to Rundstedt's force. It was charged with the most daring element of the plan, a co-ordinated thrust through the ravined and forested Ardennes region behind the main concentration of Allied forces, thus bypassing the formidable French Maginot defensive line. This was to be followed by a race to the undefended Channel coast, before turning to complete the encirclement. In the north, Bock was to make a diversionary attack into Belgium, where the Belgian Army was concentrated on a defensive line on the Albert Canal and Meuse River lines, and seize the strategically important fortress at Eben Emael.

Grossdeutschland was to play a major role in the offensive. Attached to Guderian's XIX Corps, it was to follow close behind the Panzer spearhead and consolidate the German gains.

The assault began on 10 May, with extensive air attacks on the Dutch and Belgian airfields and the seizure of vital river crossings by paratroops at Moerdijk. Bock's 9th Panzer Division then drove into Holland, toward the densely populated 'Fortress Holland' region were the Dutch army had concentrated. In response the French Seventh Army and the British Expeditionary Force (BEF) moved across Belgium to help the Dutch and Belgians. In Belgium, the allied armies soon fell back on a defensive line based on the Dyle River. Holland fell on the 14th, but although it initially appeared that the Allies had succeeded in their central delaying action, Rundstedt had already sprung the trap. Advancing on the central front were Army Group A was opposed by only four light cavalry divisions, the Chasseurs Ardennais, and ten hurriedly prepared infantry divisions, the main blow was delivered by Kleist's two Panzer corps, comprising seven divisions, which pushed through the Ardennes and across the Meuse with almost no losses.

The main body of Infantry Regiment *Grossdeutschland*, supported by artillery and engineers from the 10th Panzer Division, attacked through Luxemburg against the southern Belgian fortifications, while simultaneously elements of GD's 3rd Battalion landed as airborne troops. Rundstedt and his subordinate commanders learned that there was some reason for the French theory that the Ardennes was a difficult barrier for major attacks. It took all the first day to cross the undefended northern portion of Luxemburg, yet on the second day the German forces picked up momentum and neither the Belgian cavalry nor the French Army could do much

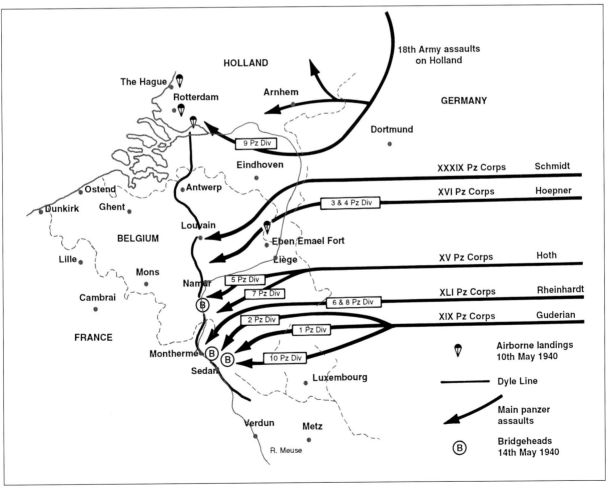

Above: Speedy river-crossing was a significant part of
Blitzkrieg. The German troops became adept at using
inflatable rubber pioneer floats to ensure early
bridgeheads when crossing wide rivers.

to stay the advance. By nightfall on the 11th Guderian's tanks had reached Bouillon on the Semois River. It was here on the next day that the regiment had its first taste of battle, skirmishing with Belgian troops whose lines had been overrun. Although a blown bridge temporarily halted the advance, a crossing was forced the next day. Continuing its advance south through Belgium, the regiment approached the Meuse at Sedan via the Forest of Sedan, Fleigneux, St Megnes and Floing, on the north bank of the river.

CROSSING THE MEUSE

In the centre of Army Group A, Guderian and Reinhardt prepared to cross the Meuse on the 13th. Reinhardt's forces at Monthermé and Mézières, and Guderian at Sedan, where the great loop in the Meuse River formed a weak spot in the French defences. In the event, the honour of forcing the first bridgehead went to Erwin Rommel's 7th Panzer Division, which crossed at Dinant at dawn on the 13th. Further south, and despite the fact that neither Guderian nor Reinhardt had built up sizeable forces for an assault crossing, an attack was ordered for the afternoon, in the hope of catching the French before they could prepare. Although the attack, supported by hundreds of aircraft, caused some panic in the French lines (manned mainly by reservists), it proved costly for the Germans. Nearly half the men in the first wave were cut down by French artillery and machine-gun fire. GD assaulted in two parts. The 7th Company to the west of the town and the main body to the east, after looping around the town of Sedan itself.

As the Germans advanced, local French commander General Huntziger launched a hasty cavalry counter-attack against the southern flank of Guderian's thrust, but 2nd Panzer was soon at the Ardennes Canal, where it seized two bridges intact.

After crossing the Meuse, IRGD was placed under the command of the 1st Panzer Division, and advanced south to Cheveuges. South of Cheveuges, the Assault Engineer Battalion split from the main body of the unit and moved west of the uplands overlooking Chémery and Bulson. Moving along the western road into Chémery, it was attacked by French tanks. The main force, having advanced through Bulson, met and held a French armoured attack south of that town.

By now the breakthrough at Sedan had seriously compromised the position of the main allied force in Belgium and, although attempts were made to eliminate the armoured penetration, none of the counter-attacks ordered over the next four days succeeded. As part of the operations to consolidate the bridgeheads over the Meuse IRGD was heavily involved in fighting with the French 55th and 61st Divisions, and 3rd Division around the Stonne highlands, south-east of Artaise, which continued over the next 48 hours. By the 19th the fighting around Bulson had begun to abate as the last tenacious defenders withdrew.

DRIVE TO THE CHANNEL

Moving with impressive speed, Kleist's armour captured St Quentin on 18 May, halfway to the Channel from Sedan, and the next day reached Amiens and Doullens, 40 miles from the coast. On May 20th Abbeville fell, and for all practical purposes the Germans now faced the Channel, having cut the BEF's line of communications with its main base at Cherbourg. On the same day as IRGD began its march towards St Omer, (south of Dunkirk) the British commander, Lord Gort, ordered the BEF to hold a line extending from south of Dunkirk to the vicinity of Arras (the 'canal line'), in an attempt to stop this rush northwards by the German forces. He attempted to drive southwards from Arras, but promised French support failed to materialise and the attack failed, in the face of determined resistance by German units, including IRGD.

Now trapped in a pocket surrounding Dunkirk, its only remaining port, pressed by Army Group A from the south along the fragile canal line and in the east by Army Group B through Belgium, where the Belgians appeared on the brink of collapse, the BEF seemed doomed. As part of Army Group A, IRGD began attacks on the British line south of Dunkirk on 24 May and by the 26th had established bridgeheads over the canal at St Pierre Brouck. That same day, the British government authorised Lord Gort to begin evacuating the BEF from Dunkirk, and the following night the BEF began withdrawing to a shallow perimeter around the port. On the 27th and 28th Wormhoudt and Herzeele were attacked, and while fighting continued south of Dunkirk, the Belgians surrendered. As has been much-debated since, Hitler halted the Panzers and entrusted the destruction of the BEF on the beaches to Goering's Luftwaffe, a decision that is seen by contemporary historians as crucially flawed. the German Army turned south, where the French held a line stretching along the Somme and Aisne rivers. This hastily constructed Weygand Line was badly compromised by the fact that during its advance to the Channel the German forces had captured vital bridgeheads on the Somme. It was to one of these, at Amiens, that the regiment was transferred on 4 June. Here, in the coastal sector, the French had concentrated their main strength, in an effort to prevent the Germans from taking the Channel ports and denying aid from Britain.

Attacks on the Weygand Line by Bock's Army Group B from north-west of Paris began on 5 June. Fighting under the temporary command of the 10th Panzer Division, itself part of Kleist's armoured group, IRGD fought alongside 86th and 69th Infantry Regiments on 6 June through the

Below: The fall of France— *Grossdeutschland* reached Lyon before the Armistice.

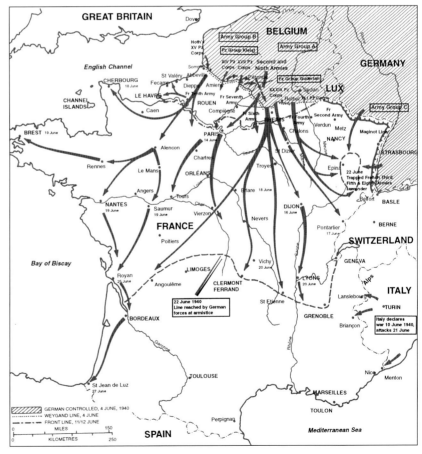

Above: Compiègne Forest, France, 21 June 1940. French envoys, accompanied by senior German officers (saluting), walk past German troops to surrender in the same railway carriage in which the 1918 Armistice had been signed by the Germans.

villages of St Fuscien and Sains-en-Amiénois, to the south of Amiens, and attacked French positions west of the Bois de Lozières on the following day. While the 1st and 2nd Battalions battled around the Bois de Lozières, the 3rd Battalion advanced to Rossignol, where it rejoined the Assault Engineer Company (which had taken Grattenpache the previous day) for a co-ordinated attack on the French defences to the north-east of the town.

Thus having helped to achieve a decisive breakthrough of the Weygand Line on 8 June, and turn the left flank of the French armies on the Aisne, the regiment began its pursuit of the French forces to the Oise River. Along the Aisne, Rundstedt launched the main attack on the 9th, and despite spirited resistance the French were forced to fall back on the Marne in deference to their open flank. On the next day Guderian's tanks broke through the line at Chalons. Subsequently, Paris was declared an open city and abandoned

IRGD was involved in further heavy fighting south of Amiens until the 10th, when Bock reached the Seine below Paris. With the destruction of the Oise Bridge much of Kleist's group was rushed to the north-east into the area around Guiscard to reinforce Army Group A. Beginning on the 13th, the regiment began a forced march to the Seine above Paris, via Coucy, Villers and Villeneuve. On the 15th, it battled for crossings over the Seine, and continued south in pursuit of the remnants of the retreating French Second and Fourth Armies. On 17 June Guderian's tanks reached the Swiss border, effectively cutting off the 500,000 French troops in the Maginot Line, and France sued for peace.

While the negotiations were underway, IRGD continued to press on south, occupying Lyon in the Rhône valley on the 19th. In and around Lyon the regiment served a month-long tenancy as the occupation force, providing a welcome opportunity for rest and relaxation. On 5 July the regiment marched to Paris and during its brief stay in the capital was reinforced with an additional company, the 17th, equipped as motorcycle troops.

On 26 July the regiment embarked for Colmar and Schlettstadt in the Alsace region, and here undertook training for Operation Seelöwe ('Sealion', the planned invasion of England) until 26 October when this was postponed indefinitely. During this period the regiment underwent much reorganisation. The Heavy Transport Battalion became the 17th and 20th Companies, and at the beginning of September a motorised artillery unit (400. Artillerie-Abteilung) was attached. The next month, a motorised engineer company was added as the 18th Company.

Between the end of October and the new year, the regiment was transferred to a training camp at Le Valdahon, near the Swiss border and here underwent training for Operation Felix—the planned assault on Gibraltar (also cancelled). In November its ranks were further swelled by the addition of a motorised flak company (20th Company).

Infanterie-Regiment *Grossdeutschland* ended 1940 with a reputation hard won on the battlefields of France. It had been involved in many of crucial actions and in them shown the quality of its men and training. The cost was not light. At the start of the western offensive the regiment numbered some 3,900 men and at its conclusion 1,108 of those had become casualties (221 killed, 830 wounded, 57 missing).

Above: Bringing food to his comrades in front-line units, this *Essentrager* (provisions' carrier) is an *Obergefreiter* (Corporal) who has been awarded the Iron Cross 2nd Class. Armed with a rifle he crouches low as he crosses open ground. Strapped to his back is the metal container holding the food.

1941: OPERATION BARBAROSSA

The losses of men and materiel in France were made good during the summer and winter months of 1940–41, during which time there was ample opportunity for new recruits to be trained, and new equipment tested. Although costly, the fighting in France had given *Grossdeutschland* a core of experienced combat veterans whose experience and camaraderie would be vital in the first year of the Russian campaign.

After overwintering at the Le Valdahon training camp on the Swiss border, in the early months of the new year *Grossdeutschland* rotated between the Le Valdahon and the nearby Belfort training camps for a period of intensive training. Unbeknown to all but a few senior officers, this was in preparation for Operation Barbarossa, the invasion of Russia.

As early as June 1940, Hitler had become convinced of the strategic value of an attack on the Soviet Union, firstly as a means of denying Britain a potential ally (and persuading her obstinate people to accept a negotiated peace), secondly as a means of acquiring *Lebensraum*—'living space'—which ostensibly was one of the reasons for the war, and lastly because he was convinced of the Soviet Union's expansionist ambitions in Europe. The OKH began planning for the invasion from that time, and this process gathered increasing impetus as hopes for a swift victory over Britain diminished.

YUGOSLAVIA

In the spring of 1941 Hitler decided to invade Yugoslavia and Greece. The Soviet Union, still Germany's ally at the time, tore up its non-aggression and friendship pacts with those two countries on 5 April and the next day German forces invaded. Beginning on 4 April *Grossdeutschland* was transported by rail from Belfort to Vienna, and from there advanced via Raab, Budapest and Szegedin to Romania. Here it was attached to the XLI Panzer Corps, which was ordered to converge on the Yugoslav capital, Belgrade, from the north-east. The regiment marched into the country on 11 April, via Arad and Temesvar, but met with little resistance from the Yugoslav Army, elements of which it pursued to the vicinity of the Danube River near Pancevo. In the early evening of the 11th an SS lieutenant hoisted the Swastika over the German legation in Belgrade and the next day German armoured spearheads entered the city. Following in their wake, 1st Battalion IRGD, took part in the occupation of the city and from then until the middle of July it acted as security troops in the regions east of the Danube—Weilka, Kikinda and Wertschetz.

RUSSIA

The occupation of Yugoslavia and Greece forced Hitler to revise the original start date of the Russian invasion (15 May), instead scheduling it for end of June. In the middle of May, the regiment received orders to move by rail to the Freudentstadt–Troppau area in south-eastern Germany. Here it remained until 15 June, when further orders came to move to the area south-east of Warsaw, around the town of Zelechów. This would be the start point for the invasion, for which it was attached as a reserve to the Second Panzer Group. Panzer groups had succeeded the highly-successful Panzer corps of the French campaign and were in fact mobile armies, but lingering conservatism among the general staff prevented their being accorded the status of fully-fledged armies. Four of them were available on the eve of the invasion, for which Germany had some 3,050,000 men, plus

Below: A half-tracked 37mm light Flak gun platoon, supported by machine-gun cover, keep a wary eye open for enemy aircraft. In the summer of 1941, following the prophylactic Luftwaffe strikes, there was little Soviet air activity.

another 750,000 from Finland and Romania, 3,350 tanks, 7,184 artillery pieces, and 600,000 motor vehicles. These were organised into three Army Groups, North, Centre and South, with support from over 3,000 aircraft. Though all of the German leaders agreed that the war hinged on the use of the Panzer groups, acting independently ahead of the infantry, Hitler was persuaded for the Russian campaign that though the Panzer corps should remain at the spearhead, they were to be in closer co-operation with the infantry in battles of the classic encirclement pattern that aimed at netting the Soviet forces before they could retreat behind the Dnieper.

On 22 June this huge force was unleashed on a 1,800-mile front against the Soviet Union, whose armies were totally unprepared to meet the onslaught. *Grossdeutschland*, marching from Zelechów as part of Bock's Army Group Centre, crossed the border on the 27th/28th in the wake of the Panzers of the 7th Division, and moved toward the objective, Moscow.

Advancing from Bialystock on the 29th, the regiment fought consolidating actions at Slonim against Soviet troops that had been encircled during the rapid advance, and launched another major drive from Baranovichi on 3 July over the northern fringes of the impassable Pripet Marshes towards Minsk. Here another large encirclement yielded more than 150,000 Soviet prisoners. Continuing the drive east, IRGD fought a major engagement at Borisov on the Beresina River, where Napoleon had crossed during his disastrous campaign of 1812. Had the men of *Grossdeutschland* peered down into the water they might have seen the timber supports of the bridges Napoleon's engineers had built. As the regiment advanced deeper into Russia, fighting became more frequent along the route, which took it up to the Dnieper north of Mogilev.

Here IRGD met with the armoured spearhead, and was assigned to the 10th Panzer Division for the assault across the river. After forcing a crossing on 11 July, fighting for the bridgehead continued for the following five days. Having broken out of the bridgehead on the 16th the regiment continued to advance in support of the XLVI Panzer Corps into the area west of Mstislavl near Yelnya, where it attacked

Above: PzKpfw IIIs and motorised infantry line up for the march during the early stages of the war in the East.

Right: The attack on Russia—the speed of the early advances, the unpreparedness and inferiority of the enemy and the culture of victory fostered by the successes of the early war years all contributed to what seemed like a perfectly executed operation. However, attrition—particularly to NCOs and junior officers—fatigue and, as Napoleon had discovered, the Russian winter held up the Germans sufficiently for the defences to be reorganised. The length of German supply lines, resolute defence and the quality of Russian armour—particularly the T-34—would prove too much for the Wehrmacht in the end.

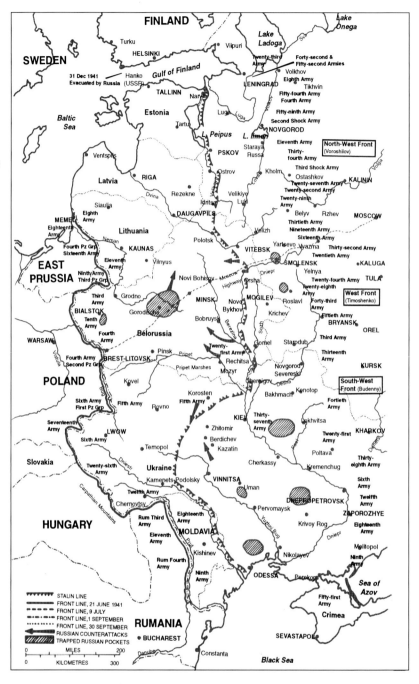

Russian positions on 21 and 22 July. On 30 July the regiment took part in the attack on the road north toward Dorogobuzh, which met with strong resistance at Ustinova. These battles and other actions at the railroad crossing south of Yelyna, at Vaskovo, raged in summer heat for the last week of July and into August. After more than a month in the front line, the regiment was afforded two days rest in the Dankovo–Vaskovo area from 6 to 8 August, and after moved into defensive positions to hold the salient that had been put into the Soviet line west of Yelyna by the 360-mile-wide advance of Army Group Centre. The capture of Smolensk on 7 August had brought 850,000 Russian captives, and towards the end of the

116

month the ferocious fighting in the vicinity of Vaskovo–Chochlovka–Rudnaya began to slacken off.

The beginning of the campaign in Russia had been characterised by rapid advances as far as the area south of Smolensk, with the fighting sporadic and small scale. Advances across the flat, empty, coverless terrain of central Russia had to be made with the support of artillery and armour and here the regiment's assault gun and artillery units proved invaluable.

On the southern front the fighting had been more intense, and better-prepared Soviet defences had held up the advance of Rundstedt and Kleist. Against the better judgment of his senior staff, who felt the maximum effort should be directed against Moscow, but encouraged by their confident predictions that the war was already won, Hitler decided to send some of Army Group Centre to the south to assist in the actions against Budyonny's West Front at Kiev. On 25 August, the Second Army and the Second Panzer Group turned southward from the Army Group Centre flank. IRGD marched south on 1 September, travelling via Roslavl, Lukaviza, and Starodub. Crossing the Desna River at Novgorod-Severskiy, it was engaged in battles to the north-east of the city to establish a secure bridgehead and, having done so, advanced further south to Glukhov by 8 September. The next day it assaulted across the Seym River at Putivl, but was checked in the bridgehead by strong resistance until the 13th. Pushing on south, the regiment fought at Schilkova, Konotop and Belopoyle, on the north flank of what was now Timoshenko's West Front. The advance was slowed by rain and mud but by the 16th the lead elements of the Second Army and the First Army, which had moved northward from the Dnieper bend, met 150 miles east of Kiev. Kiev fell on the 19th, and seven Soviet armies inside the pocket were captured. In addition to those lost at Uman in the south, this amounted to nearly 1,500,000 men, or half of the current active strength of the Soviet Army.

In the line east of Romny IRGD checked attempts by the Soviets to counter-attack between 26 September and 3 October, and on the 4th began the march back to the Roslavl area, transiting via Konotop and Gomel, and then proceeded on to Karachev, where it bivouacked in positions north of the city on 12 October.

OPERATION *TAIFUN* (TYPHOON)

Ordered by Hitler to recommence the attack on Moscow, Bock had advanced east on 2 October, encircling Bryansk and Vyazma and capturing 663,000 more Soviet prisoners. As the autumn rains set in, slowing the advance to Moscow to a crawl, IRGD was allowed a welcome period of rest and recuperation at Orel on the Oka River. Starting on the 23rd, it marched through the cloying mud to a bivouac area north-east of Mtsensk, in preparation for the following day's attack on strongly fortified Soviet positions in the area. In the last week of October, with temperatures falling ominously, IRGD ground on to Tula, less than 90 miles from Moscow, fighting many actions en route.

To the north-west, German forces were within 40 miles of the Russian capital on 20 October, but their advantage was already running out. Georgi Zhukov had arrived to take charge of the defence of the city, reinforcements were expected from the Far East, and most of the surviving Soviet warplanes were being concentrated around the city. This combination of factors held back the stab at Moscow via Tula on 15 November by Guderian's tank forces in which IRGD played a major role, fighting around Yefremov and Tula.

At the end of the month, an attempt was made to encircle Tula from the north. The regiment assaulted the Soviet defensive lines at Ryazan and Kashira to the east, but was repulsed and lost most the 17th Company (Motorcycle) at Kolodesnya. By 5 December most of the German troops had reached the limit of their endurance, and vehicles were almost inoperative in the severe weather conditions.

On 7 December Zhukov chose his moment to launch a major counter-attack on a 65-mile front against Bock's exhausted Army Group Centre forces. In the lines around Yefremov and Tula, IRGD, now on the defensive, repelled the attacks for two weeks, and then was ordered north again, to the area around Bolkhov north of Orel.

Although his troops were unprepared and poorly equipped to fight through a Russian winter, Hitler refused to allow any retreat, calling instead for fanatical resistance from his men. However, under the weight of the Soviet offensive, the German spearheads north and south of Moscow quickly crumbled, and the offensive expanded until nearly the whole of the Army Group Centre front was aflame. Fighting on the defensive on the Oka River and north of Bolkhov during the last week of the year, IRGD was called on again to reinforce weak points in the line. The regiment was spilt into units and assigned to assist three separate infantry divisions, as Soviet breakthroughs in the north and south threatened the encirclement of the entire Army Group Centre.

Although it had survived, the year has been hard for IRGD. The regiment had fought, and survived, through the extremes of the Russian summer and autumn, and was enduring its winter. Nine hundred of its men had been killed, including many experienced NCOs and enlisted men, and over 3,000 others wounded.

1942: THE FURTHEST EAST

The new year promised a different Soviet Army, one with combat experience, better tanks, guns and planes, and a growing flow of supplies from the US and United Kingdom. Behind the German lines, the partisan forces were becoming a serious threat to the overstretched supply routes, which crossed hundreds of miles of overrun but not conquered territory. During the winter, in Berlin, recriminations for the failure of the Moscow campaign were swift and unflinching. Hitler appointed himself as direct C-in-C of the Army, and 35 leading generals, including all of the Army Group leaders and Guderian and Höppner, were dismissed.

Through early 1942, with men and machines all but immobilised by the weather, IRGD was engaged in small scale fighting on the Oka River between Orel and Belev. Around Gorodok, the regiment fought for ten days to contain an attempted enemy breakthrough launched on 20 January, with the added diversion of partisan action in the forested areas around the town. Fighting to secure the area around Gorodok continued into February, but the regiment was by this time seriously depleted. Already, on 2 February, the 3rd Battalion had been disbanded and its men and equipment used to bolster the remaining battalions. On the 9th, the regiment attacked Verch as part of the operation to clear the Bolkhov–Yagodnaya railroad. Advancing on the north side of the railroad through Novoiginsky, Gorodok, and Fondeyevka, the 1st and 2nd Battalions reached Gorizy on the 15th. Casualties were again heavy, and on the 19th the two remaining Grenadier battalions were reformed into one unit. Another attack followed, this time on Kosovka and Chuchlova, and thereafter the regiment fought consolidating actions in the area while it was reorganised and brought up to strength.

Above right: The *Kettenkrad*, a versatile half-tracked motorcycle, pulling a trailer in the mud of a Russsian autumn. Behind is a Panzerjäger 38(t), a 75mm Pak 40 mounted on a PzKpfw 38(t) chassis.

Below right: The autumn rains swiftly turned the summer dirt and dust into axle-deep cloying mud making most dirt roads almost impassable, reducing movement to 'push and pull' speed.

INFANTRY DIVISION GROSSDEUTSCHLAND

Between 1 April and 22 May 1942 IRGD underwent wholesale reorganisation and expansion from a regiment into a motorised infantry division. The current *Grossdeutschland* regimental commander, Oberst 'Papa' Hoernlein was promoted to Generalmajor and given command of the new Infanterie-Division (mot) *Grossdeutschland*.

As part of the expansion into a division, new units were assigned to *Grossdeutschland*, which were formed at the Infantry School at Döberitz, Juterborg, and Wandern/Mark Brandenburg during April and May. Underlining its status as an elite unit, new recruits had to conform to exacting physical and mental standards before they could be accepted. The High Command also ordained that *Grossdeutschland* should receive the latest and the best equipment, as it became available.

On 9 April the veterans of the old regiment were relieved and travelled to Orel, and then on the 15th on to Rechitsa on the Dnieper River for a period of rest and refitting. At the beginning of May, the GD Replacement Battalion was reformed as a regiment and transferred from Neuruppin to Cottbus and the following month was expanded again to brigade size. In the last week of May the fresh units to expand GD to a division arrived by truck and rail. Infanterie-Division *Grossdeutschland* (IDGD) was then assigned to XLVIII Panzer Corps, for the summer campaign season. During June the division trained as a unit in the Fatesch area and assembled close to Shchigry for the summer offensive planned for southern Russia.

During the spring Hitler, now in direct and complete control of all operations on the Eastern Front from his headquarters at Rastenburg, outlined his plans for the summer. He ordained that these would be based on a full-scale offensive but only in the south, toward the Don River, Stalingrad and the Caucasus oilfields, the capture of which he saw as the decisive stroke. Hitler's plan was for a series of successive converging attacks; the first phase, in which IDGD would make its combat debut, was to be an enveloping thrust on the Kursk–Voronezh line, which

Above: Soldiers from *Grossdeutschland* probing through the outskirts of a Russian town: another house-to-house clearance awaits.

Below: Hot soup being ladled out from a container into individual mess tins. The men in front-line units took it in turn to collect the rations for themselves and their immediate comrades so as to avoid all the troops leaving their positions at the same time.

INFANTRY DIVISION (MOT) *GROSSDEUTSCHLAND*
as at 16 May 1942

Div HQ with Staff and Mapping Pl

GD Grenadier Regiment

Regt HQ
- 1 x Sig Platoon
- 1 x Engr Platoon
- 1 x MC Platoon

- 3 x Battalions
  Bn HQ
  - 3 x Inf Coys
  - 1 x MG Coy
  - 1 x Hy Coy
    - 1 x Engr Platoon
    - 1 x Inf Gun Section
    - 1 x PzJg Section

GD Panzer Troop
- 1 x Armd Staff Coy
- 3 x Med Armd Coys
- 1 x Armd Maint Platoon

GD Signals Bn
- 1 x Armd Radio Coy
- 1 x Armd Telephone Coy
- 1 x Lt Sigs Supply Col

GD Motorcycle Battalion

Bn HQ
- 1 x AC Platoon
- 1 x AC Coy
- 1 x Halftrack Coy
- 2 x MC Coys
- 1 x Hy Coy
  - 1 x Engr Platoon
  - 1 x PzJg Platoon
  - 1 x PzJg Sect
  - 1 x Inf Gun Sect

GD Fusilier Regiment

Regt HQ
- 1 x Sig Platoon
- 1 x Engr Platoon
- 1 x MC Platoon

- 3 x Battalions
  Bn HQ
  - 3 x Inf Coys
  - 1 x MG Coy
  - 1 x Hy Coy
    - 1 x Engr Platoon
    - 1 x Inf Gun Section
    - 1 x PzJg Section

SP Flak Company
(8 x 20mm, 2 x Quad 20mm)

(mot) Heavy Infantry Gun Coy
(2 x 150mm, 6 x 75mm)

SP Panzerjäger Coy
(9 x 75mm Pak 40)

GD Sturmgeschütz Bn

Bn HQ
- 3 x Btys of 7 assault guns

GD Artillery Regiment (mot)

Regt HQ
- 1 x (mot) Staff Coy
- 1 x (mot) Observation Coy
- 10th Nebelwerfer Bty

- 2 x Battalions
  - 1 x (mot) Bn HQ Coy
  - 2 x 105mm Btys
  - 1 x 150mm Bty

- 1 x Battalion
  - 2 x 150mm Btys
  - 1 x 100mm Bty

1 x Flak Battalion
- 3 x (mot) Btys
- 2 x SP Btys

GD Pioneer Bn
- 3 x (mot) Pioneer Coys
- 1 x (mot) lt Bridging Col
- 1 x (mot) lt Supply Col

GD Panzerjäger Bn
- 2 x (mot) Coys
- 1 x SP Coy

Supply Train
- 10 x (mot) lt Supply Cols
- 4 x (mot) hy Supply Cols
- 4 x lt Fuel Supply Cols
- 3 x (mot) Maint Coys
- 1 x (mot) lt Supply Coy

Admin Services
- 1 x (mot) Div QM Pl
- 1 x (mot) Butcher Coy
- 1 x (mot) Bakery Coy
- 1 x (mot) Fd Post Office
- 1 x MP Coy

Medical
- 3 x Ambulance Cols
- 2 x (mot) Med Coys

There were a number of differences between the old Schützen (rifle) regiments and the new Panzergrenadier Regiment. First, it was planned to equip at least the first two battalions with Sd Kfz 251s, but due to the severe shortage of production, only the first battalion of one regiment was carried by Sd Kfz 251z. The troops of the second battalion had to be transported by trucks and were nicknamed '*Gummi Panzergrenadieren*' ('rubber Panzergrenadiers'). Thus, only the first battalion was capable of following Panzers across country and fighting from their vehicles. Although the second battalion was still trained in tank-infantry tactics, its vehicles were not always able to move cross-country, so it was often held in reserve until required.

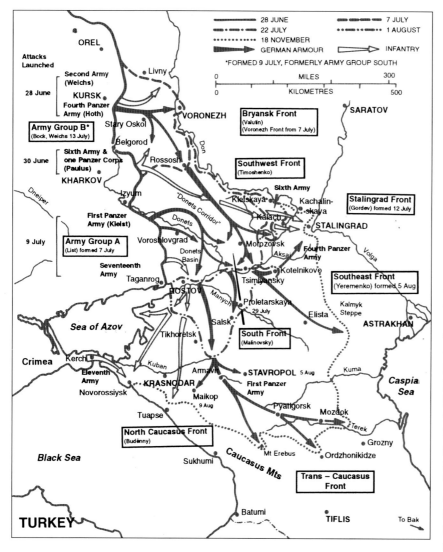

28 JUNE		7 JULY	
22 JULY		1 AUGUST	
18 NOVEMBER			
GERMAN ARMOUR		INFANTRY	

*FORMED 9 JULY, FORMERLY ARMY GROUP SOUTH

0 — MILES — 300

0 — KILOMETRES — 500

OREL

Attacks
Launched

28 June

Second Army
(Welchs)

KURSK
Fourth Panzer
Army (Hoth)

Army Group B*
(Bock, Weichs 13 July)

30 June

Sixth Army &
one Panzer Corps
(Paulus)

KHARKOV

Livny

Stary Oskol

VORONEZH

Belgorod

Rossosh

SARATOV

Bryansk Front
(Valutin)
(Voronezh Front from 7 July)

Southwest Front
(Timoshenko)

Dnieper

Izyum

Kletskaya

Sixth Army

Kachalin-
skaya

Stalingrad Front
(Gordev) formed 12 July

9 July

First Panzer
Army (Kleist)

Army Group A
(List) formed 7 July

Seventeenth
Army

Taganrog

Voroshlovgrad

Donets
Basin

ROSTOV

"Donets Corridor"

Donets

Kalacu

Morozovsk

Aksai

STALINGRAD

Fourth Panzer
Army

Volga

Kotelnikovo

Southeast Front
(Yeremenko) formed 5 Aug

Tsimlyansky

Manych

Proletarskaya
29 July

Sea of Azov

Tikhoretsk

Salsk

South Front
(Malinovsky)

Elista

Kalmyk
Steppe

ASTRAKHAN

Crimea

Kerch

Eleventh
Army

Novorossiysk

KRASNODAR

Armavir

Maikop
9 Aug

Kuban

STAVROPOL 5 Aug

First Panzer
Army

Kuma

Caspia
Sea

Tuapse

Pyatigorsk

Mozdok

North Caucasus Front
(Budenny)

Terek

Grozny

Ordzhonikidze

Black Sea

Sukhumi

Caucasus Mts

Mt Erebus

TURKEY

Batumi

Trans – Caucasus
Front

TIFLIS

To Bak

would carry the German front to the Don River.

The Soviet High Command, which had also planned to take the initiative when the good weather returned, launched a disastrous attack on the Southwest Front toward Kharkov on 12 May. Although initially successful, it met with strong German resistance and on 25 May the Germans sealed off the pocket and netted 240,000 prisoners. The plans for a Soviet summer offensive during 1942 collapsed at a stroke.

A month later, on 28 June, the Second and Fourth Panzer Armies opened the German summer offensive. Attached to the Fourth Panzer Army, GD advanced east from positions around Shchigry through Russian positions at Ivanovka and moving through Mikhailovka, Paklanovka, and Manssurovo quickly pushed through the inner flanks of the Bryansk and Southwest Fronts. The armoured spearhead reached the upper Don River on the outskirts of Voronezh on 2 July. *Grossdeutschland* assaulted across on the 5th and took the city the next day. After regrouping on the western bank of the Don, IDGD

Above: Into the Caucasus—campaigns in the second half of 1942.

marched south-east on the 8th, across the wide arc of the Don west of Kharkov, to Olchovskii on the Olchovaya.

Although he had originally planned to execute a large encirclement inside the Don bend, on the 13th Hitler ordered Army Group A (to which he attached the Fourth Panzer Army) to turn south, cross the lower Don and force the Soviet forces into a pocket around Rostov. During this advance south encounters with the enemy were limited to light skirmishing near to Tazinskaya and, after an exhausting five-day forced march in the dust and heat of summer, the division reached and crossed the Donets at Mikhailovskii on the 20th. GD then began a rapid advance south across the complex river system east of Rostov, where the Donets, Don, Sal and Manych Rivers meet. Between 21 and 23 July it fought for control of Razdorskaya on the Don. Rostov fell on the 23rd, but its capture did not produce the expected large number of prisoners. Hitler issued a new directive setting forth new objectives, ordering Army Group A to fan out south of Rostov, secure the Black Sea coast and capture the oilfields at Maikop and Grozny. At the same time the army group would have to relinquish all of its artillery and nearly half of the divisions for operations elsewhere.

In the last week of July IDGD battled to consolidate the bridgehead over the Don, which was secured by taking Susatzki. By the 31st it had advanced to the Manych River, and there was relieved. Reassembling at Razhny in early August, the division began transferred by rail to Smolensk on the 16th. In mid-August the Soviets launched major counter-attacks in the Rzhev area, west of Moscow, and GD was ordered to move north to meet the threat. South of Rzhev the division made camp, detailed as army reserve for Ninth Army, until 9 September. The next day it was plunged into one of the most savage battles yet fought on the Eastern Front, meeting a Soviet advance south of the Rzhev railroad at Ssuchtino, Tschermassovo, Vekschino and Michoyevo, which dragged on into early October at heavy cost.

On 1 October the divisional infantry regiments were renamed, in accordance with the restructuring program detailed above. The 1st Regiment became Grenadier-Regiment *Grossdeutschland* and the 2nd became Füsilier-Regiment *Grossdeutschland*. (See organisation table on page 29.)

After the bitter fighting south of Rzhev, the division was relieved on 9 October and transferred to the rest area around Olenino. Here it stayed until 25 November, during which time a ski battalion was organised for the division.

During the summer of 1942 the Red Army carried through a reorganisation of its command system, and built up overwhelming strength. On 19 November the Russians launched their second winter offensive, which aimed primarily at relieving the siege at Stalingrad. Attacking north and south of the city, they encircled the German Sixth Army and half of the Fourth Panzer Army.

While the main actions of the winter were fought in the south, bitter fighting also ensued on the northern sector. Attacks on the German Ninth Army, which was stretched over a 60-mile front from Rzhev to Byeloy west of Moscow, resumed in late November. In the sector held by Grenadier-Regiment GD, in the Lutschessa Valley, the Soviet 185th Division attacked in force south of Griva on 27 November, and made major inroads via Karskaya and Gontscharova. South of Byeloy, the Füsilier-Regiment GD (Kampfgruppe *Kassnitz*) met and held the left flank of the Soviet 35th Tank Brigade where it broke through the line at Turovo.

In the centre and on the right flank the Soviets broke through at Dubrovka and Demechi, and the regiment suffered heavy casualties trying to contain the advance. In the Lutschessa Valley, fierce fighting continued throughout the first week of December, as the German XXIII Army Corps battled to contain the Soviet drive. By the middle of the month, the battle had begun to ease and the front stabilised.

Regrouping its scattered units, the GD staff was able to count the very heavy cost of the fighting. Rushed in to stop up the breach by the High Command, which had begun to have unrealistic expectations of *Grossdeutschland*'s capabilities, the division had been almost decimated. The lull in fighting was thus something of a blessing, but it was only a brief respite. On 21 December a counter-attack was mounted with the 12th Panzer, followed by another on the 30th.

During 1942 *Grossdeutschland* lost some 10,000–12,000 of its soldiers, and twice, during February and December, came close to collapse. All that remained of the proud unit was a hard core of veterans, and the knowledge that yet more was to come.

1943: THE LONG RETREAT

During the winter of 1942–43 the tide of the war began to turn against Germany, which now found itself contending on all fronts with an enemy better led, well supplied and with a vastly greater capacity to replace losses of men and materiel. Increasingly, the German Army on the Eastern Front was engaged in defensive action, and *Grossdeutschland* was time and again called on to reinforce weak points in the German lines. Furthermore, by now the best Russian aircraft and tanks had achieved a parity with German equipment, which in the coming battles would test the German forces to the limit.

On 14 January, with nearly 300,000 Germans still trapped in the Stalingrad pocket, the Russians moved up the Don for the second time, this time to strike the Hungarian Second Army. The Hungarians soon collapsed, opening a 200-mile front between Voronezh and Lugansk (Voroshilovgrad). They then turned southwards to the Donets, threatening to envelop the remnants of Army Group B and Army Group Don, which was still battling to keep open Army Group A's lifeline to the west at Rostov.

Having stabilised the front at Rzhev, GD marched south to Smolensk, from where, on 17 January, it travelled by rail to the Volchansk area between Byelgorod and Kharkov. At this time the motorcycle units were reorganised as the Aufklärungs-Abteilung (Reconnaissance Group), and IV. Artillerie-Abteilung *Grossdeutschland* was formed at Guben in Germany.

Between 21 January and 8 February, GD fought in the Volchansk battles between the Oskol and the upper Donets River east of Byelgorod. On 25 January the Russians struck northward once more to hit the German Second Army, which was already withdrawing from Voronezh, and in three days encircled two of its three corps. Holding positions to the north and south of Volchansk respectively, the Füsilier-Regiment (Kampfgruppe *Kassnitz*) and Grenadier-Regiment (Kampfgruppe *Platen*) struggled to contain the Soviet advance but were slowly pushed back. On 3 February the lead elements of Kampfgruppe *Pohlmann* of the Führer Escort Battalion were returned to the division, and engaged at Ssurkovo north-east of Volchansk.

Stalingrad was taken by the Russians on 2 February, and Byelgorod on the 8th.

As the Soviet offensive gathered pace, the right flank of Army Group B was forced to withdraw. Between 9 and 14 February GD was involved in the fighting along the Byelgorod–Kharkov railroad, one of the vital communications links to Army Group Don and Army Group A. After the evacuation of Kharkov on the 15th, a 100-mile gap opened between the right flank of Army Group B and Army Group Don, through which Soviet units struck southward and westward across the Donets,

Above right: Wearing snow camouflage coveralls, German infantry shelter beside snow-covered trees and observe a Soviet tank burning in the middle distance.

Below right: In the metre-deep snow which makes the forests in the East almost impenetrable during the winter months, skis and snowshoes were essential but in short supply.

Opposite page, above: Wearing improvised snow camouflage, *Grossdeutschland* troops trudge through snow-covered countryside during an exercise. The lead man is carrying an MG 34 in its light—ie on a bipod—role.

Opposite page, below: A three-man machine-gun crew using the MG 34 in its heavy role on a tripod.

Above: The *Raupenschlepper Ost* (the eastern caterpillar tractor) towing 10.5mm le FH 18/40 light field howitzers to a new position. These tractors proved very useful vehicles that could overcome almost any difficult terrain and obstacle.

Left: Wearing winter camouflage, a telephone wire patrol with messenger dog carefully checks the wires.

moving to cut the remaining communications lines. Between the 16th and 23rd, GD fought to keep the Kharkov–Poltava line open. However, to the south the Donetsk railroad was cut and on the 19th the Soviets had reached the Sinelnikovo railroad junction 20 miles east-south-east of Dneperopetrovsk.

On 24 February GD was relieved and travelled to a rest area some 18 miles west of Poltava. Here it was rested and re-equipped. The newly formed 4th Artillery Battalion arrived, and so, too, the first detachment of Tiger I tanks. In the meantime, General Manstein had initiated moves to close the gap in the German line, and made preparations for a counter-attack against Kharkov, despite the inherent risks of advancing in the spring thaw. GD marched to its starting point for the attack on 5 March, and from the 7th fought through knee-deep cloying mud toward Bogodukov, which fell four days later. The Fourth Panzer Army reached Kharkov on the 11th, trapping several Soviet divisions. After mopping up these divisions, the army took its advance 30 miles farther north and took Byelgorod, and thus regained the line of the Donets to that point. GD, which helped capture Tomarovka to the north of Kharkov on the 19th, was relieved on the 23rd and transferred back to the rest area near Poltava, where further reinforcement arrived in the form of new infantry fighting vehicles (which were in constant short supply). From March to June the division was held in reserve.

In the past two years, the coming of spring had heralded new German triumphs, but although the victory on the Donets that had ended the long winter retreat had done much to restore German morale, no German commander believed that the next summer would see significant gains.

The late spring of 1943 on the Eastern Front was quiet, affording *Grossdeutschland* time for welcome rest. On 25 April, elements of the division were transferred to the Akhtyrka area on the Vorskla River; at the beginning of May III. Abteilung, Panzer-Regiment *Grossdeutschland* was raised at Paderborn in Germany and equipped with Tiger tanks.

Below: An ingenious improvised boiler, complete with smoking chimney, enables the crew members of this Panzer III to do a spot of laundering in hot water.

DEVELOPMENT OF THE PANZERGRENADIER

From their inception, motorised infantry were a key element in the concept of armoured mobile warfare. They were required not only to accompany the Panzers over difficult terrain into action, but also provide both supportive fire power and safety against enemy infantry and anti-tank units while moving under the cover of purposed designed Schützen-Panzerwagen (SPW or riflemen's armoured vehicles).

The first experimental Panzer division was founded in 1934, and included a Schützen-Brigade (rifle brigade), one leichte Schützen-Regiment (light rifle regiment) and one Kradeschützen-Battaillon (motorcycle rifle battalion) These motorised infantry units were tasked with supporting the two Panzer regiments within the Panzer division. Transportation was by both lorry and motorcycle, partly because the Wehrmacht did not have suitable armoured transport vehicles at that time.

Independent motorised infantry units came into being in 1937, when four Infanterie-Divisions (mot) were reorganised from standard Infanterie-Divisions. The second expansion of motorised infantry divisions took place after the French campaign. At that time eight motorised infantry divisions were formed, two of them later reorganised as Panzer divisions. Other motorised infantry units came from the elite troops of both Heer and Waffen-SS, namely Infanterie-Division (mot) *Grossdeutschland*, and SS-Divisions (mot) *Leibstandarte Adolf Hitler, Das Reich, Totenkopf* and *Wiking* during 1941–42. All of these were reorganised as Panzergrenadier divisions in late 1942 and finally became Panzer divisions in late 1943.

The fighting in North Africa and Russia took a heavy toll on the motorised infantry divisions and Panzer divisions, and they were rebuilt in 1943. In June most of the motorised infantry divisions were renamed as Panzergrenadier divisions and reorganised as Type 43 Panzergrenadier divisions in September. During 1943–44 several Panzergrenadier divisions were raised by the Waffen-SS and the Luftwaffe also raised its own Panzergrenadier division.

In late 1944 Panzer-Brigades were created to try to stem the collapse of the Russian Front; these were also occasionally known as Panzer-Grenadier-Brigades. In fact they were a combination of both Panzer and Panzergrenadier arms under the same command, and became the model of the Type 45 Panzer-Division created (theoretically at least) in the last period of war.

The Panzergrenadier divisions underwent final re-organisation in 1945 when units of Panzer-Division *Grossdeutschland* were expanded into four Panzergrenadier divisions. In reality, these were divisions in name only and could be more accurately be described as Kampfgruppen (battle groups).

Although it pioneered the concept of infantry mobile warfare, the German Army was never able to complete fully the formation of Panzergrenadier units, because it was unable to produce enough armoured transport to equip even a fair proportion of the Panzergrenadier units.

Below: Panzergrenadiers on the move. The vast distances, the heat and the dust made movement during the summer months almost, but not quite, as difficult to survive and fight as during the mud-caked autumn and the frozen winter months.

Above: A pause in the fighting in the Caucasus: a PzKpfw III crew takes a short break having replenished ammunition, food and water.

Below: The plan for Operation *Zitadelle*—to chop off the Russian salient at Kursk in a characteristic double pincer.

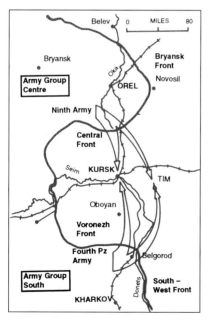

OPERATION *ZITADELLE* (CITADEL)

Although the front was now vastly extended and thinly held, Manstein's new positions offered to the German High Command the opportunity of an attack on the Soviet salient centred on Kursk. Code-named *Zitadelle*, the ensuing plan projected converging strikes on the northern and southern flanks of the salient to achieve a double envelopment. However, pre-warned of the German intentions by intelligence sources, General Zhukov was able to fortify the salient heavily. Both sides continued to build up their strength through the late spring and early summer and by the eve of the German attack some 2 million men and over 6,000 tanks were ready to go into action.

Grossdeutschland was formally redesignated as a Panzergrenadier division a week prior to the attack, on 23 June, and became almost identical in organisation to one of the elite SS Panzer divisions. During 1942 all the Army's infantry regiments had been renamed grenadier regiments and in 1943 the Infanterie-Divisions (mot) became Panzer-Grenadier-Divisions. However, the term Panzergrenadier is something of a misnomer, for in fact they were not always 'armoured', and would be better described as 'motorised infantry'.

Having been brought up to full strength for Zitadelle, the division began to the march to the staging area north of Tomarovka at the end of June 1943. The attack, launched on 4 July, saw the Ninth Army attack from the north and the Fourth Panzer Army from the south, across the base of the Soviet salient. GD attacked west of Strelazkoye with the 3rd and 11th Panzer Division, and initially made rapid advances. However, in the north the Ninth Army was stopped before a heavily fortified ridgeline on the 9th and the attack broke down, GD having advanced through the heavily defended Soviet lines as far as Kotschetovka.

On 12 July the Russians launched a strong counter-attack against the front north of Orel behind the Ninth Army. In the heavy fighting around Kalinovka, GD

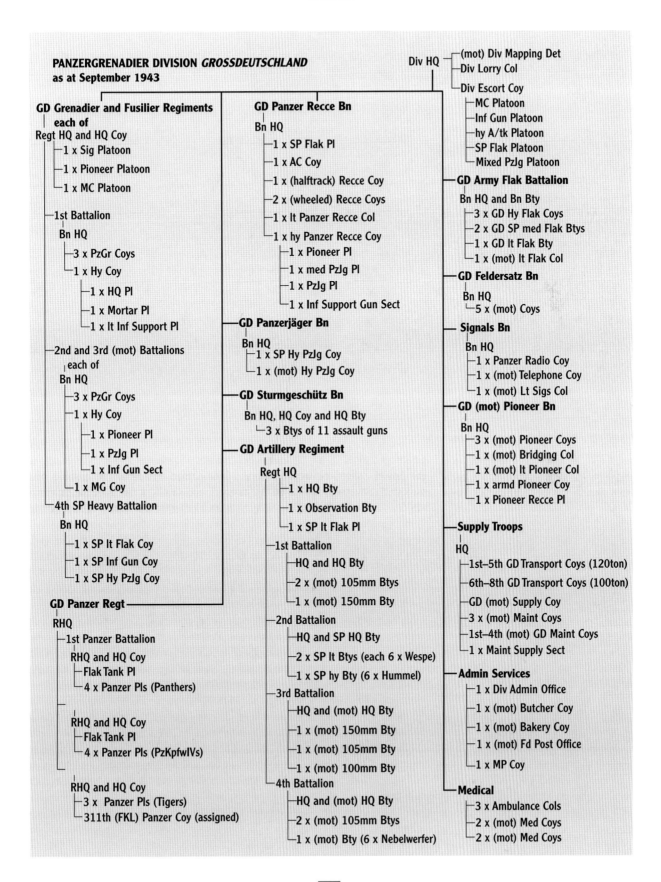

**PANZERGRENADIER DIVISION *GROSSDEUTSCHLAND*
as at September 1943**

Div HQ
- (mot) Div Mapping Det
- Div Lorry Col
- Div Escort Coy
  - MC Platoon
  - Inf Gun Platoon
  - hy A/tk Platoon
  - SP Flak Platoon
  - Mixed PzJg Platoon

GD Grenadier and Fusilier Regiments
each of
Regt HQ and HQ Coy
- 1 x Sig Platoon
- 1 x Pioneer Platoon
- 1 x MC Platoon

1st Battalion
Bn HQ
- 3 x PzGr Coys
- 1 x Hy Coy
  - 1 x HQ Pl
  - 1 x Mortar Pl
  - 1 x lt Inf Support Pl

2nd and 3rd (mot) Battalions
each of
Bn HQ
- 3 x PzGr Coys
- 1 x Hy Coy
  - 1 x Pioneer Pl
  - 1 x PzJg Pl
  - 1 x Inf Gun Sect
- 1 x MG Coy

4th SP Heavy Battalion
Bn HQ
- 1 x SP lt Flak Coy
- 1 x SP Inf Gun Coy
- 1 x SP Hy PzJg Coy

GD Panzer Regt
RHQ
- 1st Panzer Battalion
  RHQ and HQ Coy
  - Flak Tank Pl
  - 4 x Panzer Pls (Panthers)

  RHQ and HQ Coy
  - Flak Tank Pl
  - 4 x Panzer Pls (PzKpfwIVs)

  RHQ and HQ Coy
  - 3 x Panzer Pls (Tigers)
  - 311th (FKL) Panzer Coy (assigned)

GD Panzer Recce Bn
Bn HQ
- 1 x SP Flak Pl
- 1 x AC Coy
- 1 x (halftrack) Recce Coy
- 2 x (wheeled) Recce Coys
- 1 x lt Panzer Recce Col
- 1 x hy Panzer Recce Coy
  - 1 x Pioneer Pl
  - 1 x med PzJg Pl
  - 1 x PzJg Pl
  - 1 x Inf Support Gun Sect

GD Panzerjäger Bn
Bn HQ
- 1 x SP Hy PzJg Coy
- 1 x (mot) Hy PzJg Coy

GD Sturmgeschütz Bn
Bn HQ, HQ Coy and HQ Bty
- 3 x Btys of 11 assault guns

GD Artillery Regiment
Regt HQ
- 1 x HQ Bty
- 1 x Observation Bty
- 1 x SP lt Flak Pl

1st Battalion
- HQ and HQ Bty
- 2 x (mot) 105mm Btys
- 1 x (mot) 150mm Bty

2nd Battalion
- HQ and SP HQ Bty
- 2 x SP lt Btys (each 6 x Wespe)
- 1 x SP hy Bty (6 x Hummel)

3rd Battalion
- HQ and (mot) HQ Bty
- 1 x (mot) 150mm Bty
- 1 x (mot) 105mm Bty
- 1 x (mot) 100mm Bty

4th Battalion
- HQ and (mot) HQ Bty
- 2 x (mot) 105mm Btys
- 1 x (mot) Bty (6 x Nebelwerfer)

GD Army Flak Battalion
Bn HQ and Bn Bty
- 3 x GD Hy Flak Coys
- 2 x GD SP med Flak Btys
- 1 x GD lt Flak Bty
- 1 x (mot) lt Flak Col

GD Feldersatz Bn
Bn HQ
- 5 x (mot) Coys

Signals Bn
Bn HQ
- 1 x Panzer Radio Coy
- 1 x (mot) Telephone Coy
- 1 x (mot) Lt Sigs Col

GD (mot) Pioneer Bn
Bn HQ
- 3 x (mot) Pioneer Coys
- 1 x (mot) Bridging Col
- 1 x (mot) lt Pioneer Col
- 1 x armd Pioneer Coy
- 1 x Pioneer Recce Pl

Supply Troops
HQ
- 1st–5th GD Transport Coys (120ton)
- 6th–8th GD Transport Coys (100ton)
- GD (mot) Supply Coy
- 3 x (mot) Maint Coys
- 1st–4th (mot) GD Maint Coys
- 1 x Maint Supply Sect

Admin Services
- 1 x Div Admin Office
- 1 x (mot) Butcher Coy
- 1 x (mot) Bakery Coy
- 1 x (mot) Fd Post Office
- 1 x MP Coy

Medical
- 3 x Ambulance Cols
- 2 x (mot) Med Coys
- 2 x (mot) Med Coys

took heavy casualties, countering a series of Soviet armoured attacks in the second week of July. On the 17th, the division was relieved and transferred to Tamnoye to the south of the Kursk battlefield, by which point Hitler had been forced to concede defeat. Four days later GD moved again, by truck and rail, to the vicinity of Karachev, where it had fought the previous year, and was assigned to Army Group Centre.

Here it resisted the Russian advance from Bolkhov, until in early August a strong Russian attack in the south caused GD to be rushed south to join Army Group South at Akhtyrka on the Vorskla River, where the newly organised Tiger battalion joined the division. A fighting retreat along the central front continued through mid-August. The Russians had torn a 35-mile gap in the German line at Byelgorod, and through this they poured, heading south-west toward the Dnieper River. In their path, in positions to the east of Akhtyrka at Yankovka, Staraya Ryabina, Novaya Rabina and Yablotschnoye, Panzer-Grenadier-Division *Grossdeutschland* was slowly pushed back and by the 11th the men were fighting on the outskirts of Akhtyrka. At Akhtyrka, and positions to the south-east, GD battled hard, and for days with no rest, to counter the breakthrough.

Kharkov fell on 23 August, and in the last week of August the Army Group Centre front was penetrated in three places by Malinovsky's forces and Tolbukhin's Southern Front, threatening an envelopment of Army Group South. Against Hitler's orders Manstein ordered Army Group South to withdraw to the Dnieper, and in so doing probably saved it.

Reassigned to the XLVIII Panzer Corps, GD was tasked in the first two weeks of September with reinforcing the weak points in the German line to the west of Kharkov and north of Poltava. As part of the general withdrawal, the division then began a skillful fighting retreat to Kremenchug, and the vital rail bridge there over the Dnieper. Fighting behind a progressively shorter line, the division had withdrawn into a pocket around the bridge by the 29th, and then began a general withdrawal over the river (among the last German troops to do so).

GD was now in a tenuous defensive position behind the Dnieper River, the strongest natural defensive line in western European Russia (but over which the Russian had five bridgeheads). In two and a half months Army Group Centre and South had been forced back for an average of 150 miles on a front 650 miles long. In so doing, the Germans had lost the most valuable territory they had taken in the Soviet Union.

In the first week of October, the Eastern Front was relatively quiet as the Russians regrouped and brought up new forces. Their numerical superiority allowed them to rest and refit their units in shifts, and they reached the Dnieper with their offensive capability largely intact.

Below: Operation *Zitadelle* was a disaster for the German forces in Russia. After expending men and tanks on the Russian defences, all their gains were swallowed up quickly as the Russians counter-attacked.

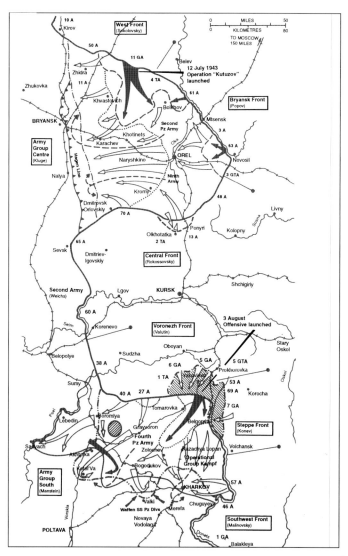

Grossdeutschland, by contrast, had little time for rest. Reforming as separate detachments, the division was engaged in defensive battles for the first two weeks of October around the Russian-held Michurin-Rog bridgehead south of Kremenchung in support of the First and Eighth Panzer Armies. The Russians threw the full weight of the Second and Third Ukrainian Fronts against these two armies on 15 October, and opened a 200-mile-wide bridgehead between Cherkassy and Zaporozhe, while to the south the Third Ukrainian Front threatened important iron and manganese mining areas near Krivoi Rog and Nikopol. Hitler was determined to hold these at all costs.

In the first week of November, Kiev was retaken by the First Ukrainian Front, and the Fourth Panzer Army was pushed back west and south of the city, threatening to destroy the entire left flank of Army Group South, along which Grossdeutschland was ranged. Beginning in the middle of October, the division carried out a long and difficult retreat south and by the end of November was established on a line that stretched from Sofiyevka to Alexandrovka, to the east of Krivoi Rog.

December brought some respite, and the German forces were able to regain some of their balance. The best solution to the German predicament at this stage would have been to order Army Group South to withdraw to the next major line of defence, the Bug River, but this Hitler would not consider. Instead the armies were told to hold their positions for the winter, and informed that they would have to do so without extra resources since these were needed for defence against the expected invasion of north-west Europe.

In the third winter of the Russian campaign, the men of Grossdeutschland could reflect on a year in which they had received little or no rest, and had time and again been used to reinforce weak points in the German lines. Higher than average losses, many of them from the experienced core of veterans, were made good with new recruits, and despite the serious deterioration on all fronts during 1943, the division was able to keep its cohesion at a time when serious manpower shortages were forcing the Germans to field half strength divisions.

Above: The original caption to this photograph boasts: 'The new German "Tiger" Panzerkampfwagen, the terror of our enemies! This tank is an outstanding achievement of the German armament technology. These steel giants clear the way on all fronts for our incomparable infantry.' Tigers were introduced to the Eastern Front around Leningrad in August 1942 and had an immediate impact on the battlefield.

1944: THE BEGINNING OF THE END

On Christmas Eve 1943, on the southern flank of the German line, the First Ukrainian Front drove into the southern rim of the Fourth Panzer Army's positions around Kiev, and the next day it developed a second thrust west. Both threatened the envelopment of Army Groups South and A, but Manstein considered the southern thrust the greater danger, and ordered the Fourth Panzer Army to stop the Soviet armies from advancing south.

Below: Russian advances in the latter part of 1943 saw the Germans lose ground extensively in the Ukraine. 1944 would be a long, hard struggle for the men of *Grossdeutschland.*

Grossdeutschland was soon in the thick of the action. Relieved at Krivoi Rog on 3 January, the unit was transferred to Kirovgrad in the path of the Soviet forces. Beginning from here it fought a continuing series of retreating defensive engagements until March. The First Ukrainian Front was approaching Uman by mid-January, but Hitler's insistence on holding the mines near Nikopol and Krivoi Rog meant that by the end of the month the Sixth Army had nearly been encircled. Also in mid-January, the 1st Battalion, 26th Panzer Regiment, equipped with Panther tanks, joined Panzer-Regiment *Grossdeutschland.* Later in the month, Generalleutnant Hoernlein, known affectionately by his troops as 'Papa', ceded command to the experienced Generalleutnant Manteuffel.

Between 27 January and 8 February a large part of the newly-reinforced Panzer-Regiment *Grossdeutschland* was transferred to the Cherkassy area, where Zhukov's First and Second Ukrainian Fronts had encircled two German corps. Together with most of Army Group South's tank strength, the unit succeeded in breaking half the trapped corps out on 17 February. Another element of the division, Kampfgruppe *Bohrend*, went to the Narva front on 5 February.

During early February the right flank of Army Group South was driven behind the 1939 Polish border nearly to Kovel. At the end of the month Army Groups South and A held a weak but almost continuous line about halfway between the Dnieper and the Bug.

In mid-February, with Army Group North retiring behind a fortified line (the Panther Line) and Army Groups South and A in comparatively stable positions, optimists in the German High

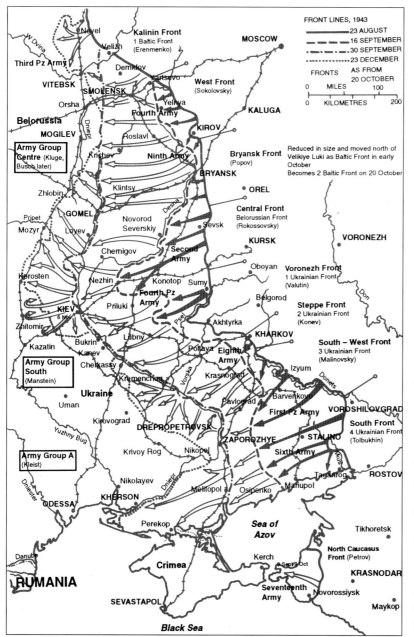

FRONT LINES, 1943
23 AUGUST
16 SEPTEMBER
30 SEPTEMBER
23 DECEMBER
FRONTS AS FROM 20 OCTOBER
0 MILES 100
0 KILOMETRES 200

Reduced in size and moved north of Velikiye Luki as Baltic Front in early October
Becomes 2 Baltic Front on 20 October

Command assumed that they had seen another winter through, and that, as in previous years, with the onset of spring, the front would sink into the mud for a month or so. The winter of 1943–44 was unusually warm and wet and therefore muddy, but even this did not prevent the Russians (whose own armour and transport, and that gifted by their Allies, were better able to move in mud) from advancing on all fronts.

During February the Soviet High Command shifted five of its six tank armies to the area opposite Army Group South, and by the end of the month another had appeared. On 4 March the First, Second and Third Ukrainian Fronts attacked the northern, central and southern flanks of Army Group South. *Grossdeutschland*, in positions west of Kirovgrad, met the onslaught of the Second Ukrainian Front, aimed at the centre of the Eighth Army east of Uman. Again the division was used to reinforce weak areas of the line, but by 15th had retreated south-west to Rovnoye.

The lack of manpower with which to meet the advance was a telling factor. So it was on all fronts. In Germany, measures were being taken to resolve the manpower crisis, but they were desperate and shortsighted. At the beginning of March, from the reinforcement forces of GD at Cottbus and Guben a Replacement Grenadier Regiment (mot) 1029 GD was raised. On 9 March, as the division withdrew under fire to the bend in the Bug River, Regiment 1029 GD transferred to Zakopane, and ten days later participated in the occupation of Hungary.

On 16 March the main body of the division began withdrawing all the way back to the Dniester River, via Pervomaisk, Ananjew, Voljadinka, and Rybniza. By the end of the month it had retreated into Romania, at Chisinau and Regiment 1029 GD was occupying Carpathian Mountain passes on the Hungarian–Romanian border at Kimpolung. The Soviets were now across the Prut River, having gained 165 miles on the three main thrust lines, and the German front was backed up against the Carpathians.

During early April, the Fourth Ukrainian Front launched an attack on the Crimea, trapping the German Seventeenth Army and forcing it into a small beachhead around Sevastopol. Despite these reversals, Germany was still far from beaten; Hitler had succeeded in his determination not to weaken the western defences for the sake of the east, German industrial output was still rising and tank and weapon production were sufficient to equip new divisions for the west and replace some of the losses in the east.

On the Carpathian front, *Grossdeutschland* fought defensive battles both east and west of Jassy in early April, during a gradual retreat to Targul Frumos in Bessarabia. The bitter fighting for the town continued for over a month, after which the front settled down to a period of relative quiet. During the respite, the Ist Battalion, Panzer-Füsilier-Regiment *Grossdeutschland* returned to Germany to equip with SPWs, and the armoured reconnaissance unit was also re-equipped. At

Above: Unloading essential equipment from an *'Tante Ju'* (Aunty Ju), a Junkers Ju52/3m transport aircraft, on an airfield somewhere on the Eastern Front.

Below: Tank recovery platoon in action. Two Hanomags attempt to pull a disabled SP gun from where it has become stuck in the mud, 26 June 1944.

the same time, however, fusilier regiments were reduced to three battalions instead of four and each battalion was reduced from five companies to four.

At the beginning of June 1944, the Führer Escort Battalion was reinforced to regimental strength in East Prussia, and the main body of *Grossdeutschland* transferred to an area north of Podul on the Dniester. Here the division, reinforced on the 6th by returning elements of the Füsilier-Regiment, launched a counter-attack against Soviet forces. As it did so, the Allies launched Operation Overlord, the invasion of Northwest Europe. 1st Battalion, Panzer Regiment *Grossdeutschland*, in France converting to Panther tanks, was quickly thrown into the fighting around the Normandy beachhead.

After the fighting around Podul, the division moved to a rest area some 60 miles south of Jassy. The Füsilier-Regiment, freshly equipped with SPWs rejoined the division, and the Armoured Assault Engineer Battalion was reformed as an Armoured Assault Regiment. The short-lived Regiment 1029 was broken up and its men used to fill gaps in the ranks of other units of the division. After more than a month in the rear, the division was transferred in late July from Romania to East Prussia, to the area around Gumbinnen.

During the rest period, an attempt was made on Hitler's life by senior army officers. Seizing control of Berlin and its government quarter remained the pivotal goal of the conspirators and the immediate focal point of Operation Valkyrie. To accomplish the coup in Berlin, the army conspirators planned to use the troops of the *Grossdeutschland* Guard Battalion in Berlin, commanded by Otto Remer, and the personnel of the Infantry School in Döberitz, the Artillery School in Krampnitz, and Potsdam's 23rd Infantry. All SS and Gestapo offices in central Berlin, and Königswusterhausen radio station were top priority targets that were to be seized in the first hours of the intended coup. However, Remer stayed loyal to Hitler and, when it became known that the Führer had survived the bomb blast, the coup collapsed.

Above: June 1944, a happy snap in front of a burning IS-2 Stalin tank of the man who knocked it out. Introduced in spring 1944, nearly 4,000 of these 122mm-armed monsters saw war service.

Above: Gunners from an artillery unit move behind their well-camouflaged howitzer to take up new positions, February 1944. Note rifle rack on rear of the 10.5mm le FH 18/40 light field howitzer.

Left: Winter in the East. Wrapped in blankets and wearing winter clothing, a mortar crew huddles in a shell crater, a shallow depression in the snow-covered terrain, trying to keep warm during a break in the fighting.

Opposite page: A typical '*Frontschweine*', fatigued by the rigours of combat. He's wearing a standard issue field grey overcoat and leather belt and harness and carries a Karabiner 98k over his right shoulder.

Hitler and his staff fully expected that the Russians would renew their pressure on the southern flank and attempt to smash Army Group North Ukraine against the Carpathians. To meet this expected advance he transferred 80 per cent of Army Group Centre's armour to the south. Instead, the Russians struck north, at Army Group Centre, which held the last major stretch of Soviet territory left in German hands between Vitebsk and Orsha. Between 22 and 25 June they made deep penetrations across the whole front, and in less than two weeks 25 of the 38 Army Group Centre divisions were lost.

In July, the Soviet offensive spread to the flanks. In the north the First Baltic Front drove into the gap between Army Groups Centre and North toward East Prussia and the Baltic. On 29 July one of the Soviet spearheads reached the Baltic west of Riga and cut off Army Group North. On the southern flank of Army Group Centre, a two-pronged thrust aimed toward Brest-Litovsk carried the Soviets to Lublin and Warsaw. Only in August did the Soviet offensive subside, having outrun its supply lines.

In early August GD began an attack east from Gumbinnen toward the vicinity of Wilkowischken (Wolfsburg) and Virballen, to take the initiative while the Soviet forces rested. The attack was a success, and Wilkowischen was taken. Soon, a new crisis arose in Lithuania, and the division marched to the area west of Schaulen (Siauliai) via Tauroggen, Kraziai, Kolainiai, and Luoke, for an attack to the east to prevent Soviet forces breaking through to the Baltic and cutting off the Kurland Front. On the 18th desperate battles to keep open this narrow land corridor to Army Group North began. Four days later, *Grossdeutschland* marched north and prepared for an attack towards Tukums, but this was halted on 25 August on the Lithuanian–Latvian border outside Doblen. After consolidating, the division then constructed defensive positions around Doblen, where it remained for the duration of September and into October.

At the beginning of September, Generalleutnant Manteuffel was replaced by Oberst Lorenz, commander of the Panzer-Grenadier-Regiment GD, and a month later the Guard Battalion in Berlin was expanded to regimental size.

Already, Army Group North had been forced to retreat to avoid being cut to pieces by an assault by the three Baltic fronts, and at the end of September had barely succeeded in escaping through the corridor south of

Right: Original German press release caption: 'The Messenger. The telephone wires have been destroyed, the radio is being used by the artillery—now is the time for a runner to get an important message to the next sector. The call "Messenger!" goes out. In the next moment he is standing in front of his company commander to receive the vital order. He knows what is at stake. In a scene reminiscent of the Great War, the Runner from the artillery unit splashes through deep muddy water at the bottom of a trench.'

Below: Russian advances in summer 1944.

Riga that GD had fought to keep open. On 3 October parts of the division began transferring to the area west of Schaulen to meet the westward drive by the First Baltic Front. In the hard fought battles around Schaulen and Memel (Klaipeda) on the Baltic coast GD fought hard, but could do nothing to prevent the Russians from breaking through to the Baltic south of Memel on the 10th, cutting Army Group North off again in the Kurland. Around Memel, GD threw up a strong defensive perimeter that it was ordered to hold for more than a month, while the rest of the army group was evacuated from the port. Panzer-Regiment *Grossdeutschland*, attached to the 6th Panzer Division, was in action during the second week of October in the Rozan area of Poland.

During the summer and autumn the German position on all fronts had become increasingly desperate. On the Eastern Front, the focus of the Soviet summer offensive had swung back to the Balkans in mid-August, succeeded in retaking the vital Ploesti oilfields at the end of the month, and ended when Romania and Bulgaria capitulated. Finally, in October Belgrade was retaken. At the same time Allied troops were pushing the Germans steadily back through north-west Europe and Italy. Launching his last major offensive of the war against the Ardennes sector on the Western Front in December, Hitler failed in his plan to split the Allied armies and in the west began the retreat to the Fatherland. (For an account of the Führer Escort Brigade's participation in the Ardennes Offensive see below.)

Right: Grossdeutschland Tigers on the road to Iasi, Romania, May 1944.

Below: The Russian advance continues into central Europe.

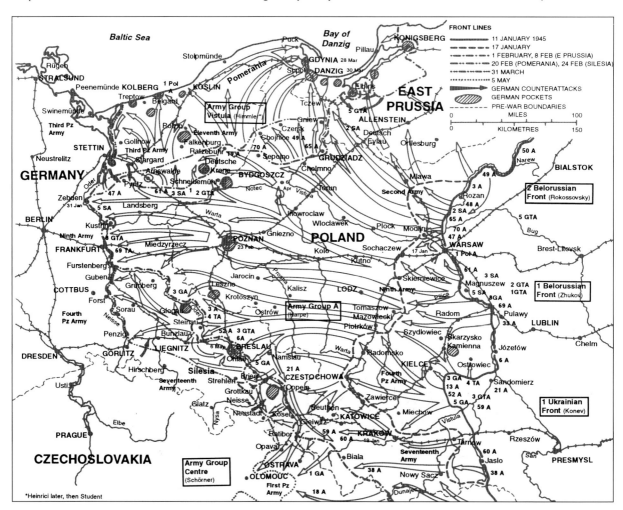

PANZER CORPS GROSSDEUTSCHLAND as at December 1944

Corps Staff
500th (mot) Mapping Det
500th (mot) MP Det
500th Recce Coy
500th (mot) Sound Ranging Pl
500th Escort Coy
500th Arty Bde Staff
500th (mot) Pioneer Regt Staff

Corps Troops
Fusilier Regt GD (2 x Bns and 1 x Inf Gun Coy)
Heavy Panzer Bn GD (HQ and HQ Coy, 1 x SP Flak PL, 3 x Tiger Coys, 1 x Maint Coy, 1 x Supply Coy)
500th Arty Regt (2 x Bns each of HQ and HQ Bty, 3 x (mot) Hy Btys)
500th Pz Pioneer Bn (HQ and HQ Coy, 3 x (mot) Pioneer Coys, 2 x (mot) Pz Bridging Cols)
44th Pz Sigs Bn (1 x Pz radio Coy, 1 x (mot) Sigs Coy, 2 x (mot) Telephone Coys, 1 x (mot) Sigs Supply Coy)
Pz Feldersatz Regt GD (2 x Bns each with 4 x Coys)

Pz Corps Support Troops (Supply Bn, Ordnance Bn, Motor Vehicle Maint Bn, Admin Troops Bn, 500th Med Bn, 500th (mot) Field Post office)

Fighting Troops
GD Panzergrenadier Division (inc PzRegt 1 of 3 Coys of 17 Panthers, PzRegt 2 of 4 Coys of 17 PzKpfwIVs) and Hy Pz Bn with Tigers.
BR Panzergrenadier Division
18th Arty Division

PANZER KORPS GROSSDEUTSCHLAND

In early November 1944 the OKH began reorganising Panzer-Grenadier-Division GD as Panzer-Korps GD by combining the division with the Panzer-Grenadier-Division *Brandenburg* (BR) and other units. It should be noted, however, that the Panzer-Korps GD never fought as a single unit, and its material strength was never comparable to that of a pre-1943 army corps.

In mid-November, the division was still holding its defensive positions around the Memel bridgehead. 1st Battalion, Panzer Regiment GD rejoined the division and 1st Battalion, Panzer Regiment 26, which had fought with GD while the former was in France, transferred to Hungary to fight attacks by the Second and Third Ukrainian Fronts against Budapest. On the 26th, the final evacuation of Memel began and GD was moved via boat through Königsberg (Kaliningrad) into the area around Rastenburg-Sensburg, to join the newly organised Panzer-Korps GD.

By the end of 1944, Germany's defeat had become inevitable. Throughout the year German forces had been almost continually on the defensive and now were fighting on home soil. GD had paid heavily in these defensive battles, and shortages in men and equipment were no longer made good. As an armoured corps, the main unit was continually pushed into the worst fighting, resulting in heavy casualties. Furthermore, the Training and Replacement Brigade had been vastly overburdened by the losses, and by the creation of the Führer-Begleit-Brigade and the Führer-Grenadier-Brigade, and as a result had virtually collapsed. To allay this crisis, the Training and Replacement Regiments of the Panzer-Grenadier-Division *Brandenburg* were attached to GD.

At the end of December of the fourth winter on the Eastern Front, *Grossdeutschland* was in camp near Hitler's headquarters at Rastenburg, resting and re-equipping for the defence of the Fatherland.

1945: THE FINAL ACT

In the first week of the new year, the division and the corps staff GD moved to the Willenberg area, where it was assigned as OKH reserve. On the 12th, Panzer-Grenadier-Division *Brandenburg* (commanded by Generalmajor Schulte-Heuthaus) was ordered to transfer to Lodz and along with the Luftwaffe Parachute Panzer Division *Hermann Göring* was placed under the command of the corps staff *Grossdeutschland*, and its commander General der Panzertruppe Saucken.

The final Soviet offensive of the war was launched on 12 January, with the bulk of the effort concentrated against the northern front, towards East Prussia, Silesia and Pomerania. Soviet leaders hoped that early and deep penetrations could then be exploited by a drive across Poland to the Oder River. From the 15th to the 30th, GD fought a series of defensive actions in northern Poland, but could not contain the advance of the Second and Third White Russian Fronts, driving west from

Below: Fatigue apparent on their faces, these troops are rotated after a period of sustained fighting.

Above: Troops reload a camouflaged six-barrelled Nebelwerfer rocket-launcher. Originally designed to lay smoke (thus the name), the 15cm Nebelwerfer 41 on a two-wheeled carriage was the main version.

Ebenrode and north-west of Warsaw, and was forced to retreat north into an area south of Königsberg in East Prussia.

During the same period, the *Brandenburg* Division was transferred to the Lodz–Piotrkov area in Poland to meet the First White Russian Front advancing south of Warsaw, but to avoid being encircled by the two arms of the attack, began retreating west out of its positions to the Neisse River north of Görlitz.

Then began a complex and ultimately fruitless period of reorganisation, as successive Panzer-Korps *Grossdeutschland* units were expanded. On 20 January the Army Tank Destroyer Force GD was formed by Panzergrenadier Replacement Brigade GD in Cottbus, and went into action on the Oder River at Steinau. The Führer-Grenadier-Brigade was transferred to a rest centre south of Arzfeld after months of heavy fighting. On 26 January Panzer-Grenadier-Division *Kurmark* (KMK) was formed from various Kampfgruppen and extemporised units of the GD Replacement Brigade (for a full account of this unit's history see below), and on the 30th the OKH ordered the Führer-Begleit-Brigade and Führer-Grenadier-Brigade expanded to full Panzer divisions, these becoming Führer-Begleit-Division (FBD) and Führer-Grenadier-Division (FGD) respectively.

At the end of January *Grossdeutschland* was engaged in heavy fighting in East Prussia, where it had retreated in the face of the Russian steamroller to positions around Bischofsburg and Braunswalde. In early May, the Guard Regiment *Grossdeutschland* became the Field Guard Regiment *Grossdeutschland* and went into action near Kustrin, while the FGD (newly refitted at Koblenz) and FBD were transferred to Stargard and Freienwalde respectively for an attack on Stargard. This was launched on 12 February, but lacking the strength that the units' spurious divisional status suggested, it was only successful in stabilising the front and captured little territory.

Above: During a pause in the fighting, the crew of a light 37mm anti-aircraft gun prepare a meal.

Above right: The Russians surround Berlin.

Below right: Two Tigers prior to a local counter-attack. This photograph gives an excellent close-up of the turret front and front of the tank. Note the machine gun, driver's armoured viewing slit and smoke dischargers on either side of the turret.

On the 12th, in recognition of the growing crisis on the Eastern Front, the 'Emergency' Brigade GD was organised at Cottbus from the GD Replacement Brigade. (It subsequently went into action at Forst on the Oder River, and was taken over by the *Brandenburg* Division on 10 March.)

The Oder was the last natural line of defence before Berlin, but by 3 February, the First White Russian Front was on the river only 35 miles east of Germany's capital. To the south, the First Ukrainian Front began attacking across the Oder north of Breslau (Wroclaw) on 8 February. What was left of the GD replacement units stationed at Guben near Görlitz were then thrown into the battles between Forst and the Czech border area, as the Panzer-Korps *Grossdeutschland* fought to contain the advance of the First Ukrainian Front to the Neisse River.

Through January and February, the *Grossdeutschland* Grenadier and Fusilier Regiments were slowly pushed back into a defensive pocket on the Fritsches Haff (Bay). By the end of March only 4,000 men remained, and on the 29th the survivors were evacuated from the port of Balga to Pillau by ferry, almost immediately going into combat in the Samland. Further south, in the last week of February, through March and into the second week of April, desperate defensive battles were fought by the *Brandenburg* Division on the Neisse River between Muskau and Steinbach.

In late March, the GD replacement units not engaged in combat were transferred to Schleswig-Holstein and Denmark. In early March, the action on the Neisse slackened, and the focus of action transferred to the south in front of Hungary. On 10 March both FGD and FBD were again relieved and transferred, to Angermünde and Langenoeis respectively. On 15 March FGD went back into combat near Stettin (Szczecin) on the Oder.

In a final flurry of reorganisation, the Panzergrenadier Combat Force *Grossdeutschland* was formed from the GD replacement forces in Denmark and Schleswig-Holstein on 23 March. PGD *Kurmark*, which had been fighting on the Oder north of Frankfurt since the end of February, was relieved and sent to rest behind the front lines on 28 March.

The Russians regrouped on the Oder-Neisse line in April, the Second White Russian Front in the north, the First White Russian in the centre opposite Berlin and the First Ukrainian Front (under Konev) in the south. This last force faced the core of GD and BR across the Neisse on the night of 15 April. The attack fell on the 16th, and in the south the division could not prevent a breakthrough by the vastly numerically superior Soviet armies on the first day.

In early April, both the FGD and FBD were transferred to Vienna, Austria. The newly created Panzergrenadier Combat Force GD entered combat at Lingen on the Ems River and was later absorbed by the 15th Panzergrenadier Division.

Although it was clear to all by mid-April that the war had now become little more than a pointless personal crusade by the Führer, the divisions continued to fight on. In the last two weeks of the month *Kurmark* engaged in very heavy defensive fighting between the Oder and Halbe, and the few remnants of GD were largely destroyed or dispersed in heavy retreating battles at Pillau. The last survivors of GD were able to cross the Hela peninsula and from there go via Bornholm to Schleswig-Holstein. FBD was destroyed in battles east of, and in the area of Spremberg, although some survivors were able to make it back to Panzer-Korps GD

BR and Panzer-Korps GD were engaged in heavy, costly defensive fighting and retreat between the Neisse River and Dresden. On 1 May BR was transferred to the Olmutz area, from where it fought to escape encirclement between the 3rd and 9th

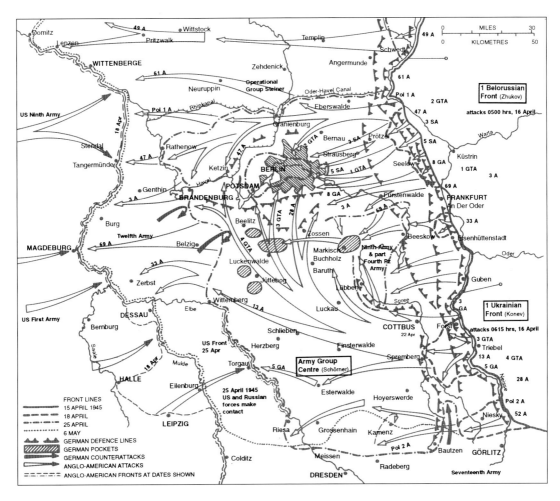

FRONT LINES
—————— 15 APRIL 1945
– – – – 18 APRIL
—·—·— 25 APRIL
············ 6 MAY
▲▲▲▲ GERMAN DEFENCE LINES
▨▨▨ GERMAN POCKETS
⟶ GERMAN COUNTERATTACKS
➡ ANGLO-AMERICAN ATTACKS
–··–··– ANGLO-AMERICAN FRONTS AT DATES SHOWN

Above: An Army flak-artillery unit—twin 37mm guns on a halftrack. An Army Flak Battalion was provided for most motorised infantry divisions from September 1943.

Right: Laying Teller mines on a muddy road in the Pripet swamp area.

Opposite page, above: Heavy self-propelled artillery fording a river somewhere on the Eastern Front, 11 May 1944.

Opposite page, below: Tigers grouping on a reverse slope for a counter-attack. *Grossdeutschland* received the Tiger before many other units, having a Tiger battalion from summer 1943.

Above: Troops snatch a mid-day meal break crouching in their trench mortar position.

Right: German grenadiers dismount from a Sturmgeschütz.

to Deutschbrod. In the battle for Berlin between 19 April and 5 May the Guard Regiment GD was all but wiped out. On the 7th Germany signed an unconditional surrender at Reims, repeating the process on the 9th in Berlin. Some 2,000,000 German soldiers passed into Soviet captivity, including most of Panzer-Korps *Grossdeutschland* and all of FGD (which was turned over under agreement after surrendering to the Americans). Those that survived Soviet captivity only returned years later.

THE PANZER DIVISION 'KURMARK'

In January 1945 following the massive Soviet offensive on the Vistula, *Grossdeutschland* Panzer Corps, along with other units from Hungary and the Western Front were ordered to bolster up the section of front in the vicinity of Fourth Panzer Army. The Soviet Army was now advancing on the Oder and such was the speed of the advance that, having raced across the Vistula, it had broken the German front line in several places. XI and XXIV Panzer Corps were sent to restore some semblance of order to the German front but the Soviets launched a strong counter-attack on the German forces and surrounded XXIV Panzer Corps. cutting it off in a pocket.

Grossdeutschland was sent to rescue the trapped units, but the front around them was crumbling. In response, the OKH was prompted to created some large Kampfgruppen to provide greater flexibility in defence. One of these new battle groups, Kampfgruppe *Langkeit* under the command of Oberst Willi Langkeit, was formed on 3 February 1945 and was made up from the Corps Panzergrenadier Replacement Brigade which was almost at full strength and Alarm Group *Schmeltzer*. It was organised as a Type 44 Panzergrenadier Division, with its Panzergrenadier battalions organised on the 1945 model, with three self-propelled gun companies equipped with Jagdpanzer 38s and one company with Pz Mk IVs. The artillery battalion was organised from the 3rd Battalion, 184th (mot) Artillery Regiment. The Panzergrenadier regiment apparently had only a staff, a staff company, and two Panzergrenadier battalions. The order of 4 February 1945 gave the division an authorised strength of 4,559 men including 128 Hiwis.

They were sent into action on 27 January at Sternberg to free the trapped German units, which included SS-Oberführer Wilhelm Bittrich's SS Panzer Corps. On 30 January Langkeit sent in the 2nd Battalion of his Kampfgruppe which, after some heavy fighting around Pinnow, made contact with the SS troops, joining up with them as they retreated towards Frankfurt. Langkeit's troops were to defend Reppen which was the position the Soviets were advancing on to outflank the main body of his battle group.

When it became evident to Langkeit that the Soviets were about to outflank him and there was no realistic chance of advancing to Sternberg he decided to move towards Reppen in order to reinforce the 2nd Battalion. This journey was hampered by refugees who clogged the roads with carts and other forms of transport and when a Soviet attack met the battle group head on many civilians died in the resulting battle. It was evident that they were almost surrounded and Langkeit ordered a breakout through the nearby woods. Again they met Soviet resistance and even an attack by a squadron of Hans Ulrich Rudel's tank-busting Stukas did not help matters much.

Eventually, on 3 February, the Soviet line was broken with the aid of tank destroyers of Langkeit's battle group and men and armour as well as some civilian refugee columns poured through the gap, all heading in the direction of Frankfurt.

PANZERGRENADIER DIVISION KURMARK AS AT 14 FEBRUARY 1945

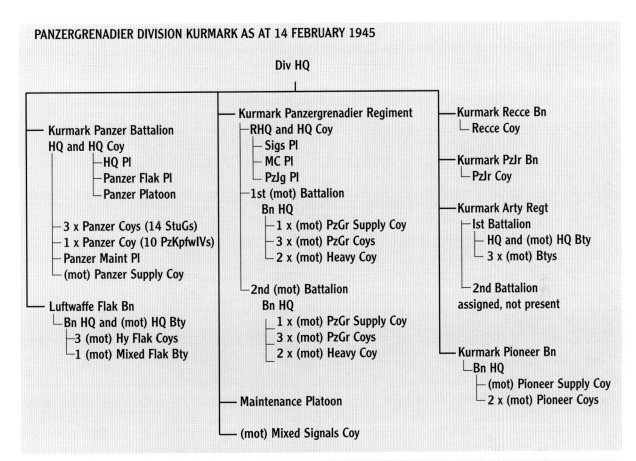

Div HQ

Kurmark Panzer Battalion
HQ and HQ Coy
- HQ Pl
- Panzer Flak Pl
- Panzer Platoon

- 3 x Panzer Coys (14 StuGs)
- 1 x Panzer Coy (10 PzKpfwIVs)
- Panzer Maint Pl
- (mot) Panzer Supply Coy

Luftwaffe Flak Bn
- Bn HQ and (mot) HQ Bty
  - 3 (mot) Hy Flak Coys
  - 1 (mot) Mixed Flak Bty

Kurmark Panzergrenadier Regiment
- RHQ and HQ Coy
  - Sigs Pl
  - MC Pl
  - PzJg Pl
- 1st (mot) Battalion
  Bn HQ
  - 1 x (mot) PzGr Supply Coy
  - 3 x (mot) PzGr Coys
  - 2 x (mot) Heavy Coy

- 2nd (mot) Battalion
  Bn HQ
  - 1 x (mot) PzGr Supply Coy
  - 3 x (mot) PzGr Coys
  - 2 x (mot) Heavy Coy

- Maintenance Platoon

- (mot) Mixed Signals Coy

Kurmark Recce Bn
- Recce Coy

Kurmark PzJr Bn
- PzJr Coy

Kurmark Arty Regt
- Ist Battalion
  - HQ and (mot) HQ Bty
  - 3 x (mot) Btys

- 2nd Battalion
assigned, not present

Kurmark Pioneer Bn
- Bn HQ
  - (mot) Pioneer Supply Coy
  - 2 x (mot) Pioneer Coys

FÜHRER BEGLEIT (ESCORT) BRIGADE as at the Battle of the Bulge

Expanded to a Brigade in November 1944, the Führer Begleit Brigade's order of battle was:

Bde HQ and HQ Coy
   (1 x halftrack Inf Pl, 1 x halftrack Flak Pl)
Brigade troops
   (1 x AC Recce Coy, 1 x Sigs Coy, 1 x Flak Coy, 1 x Pioneer Coy, 1 x SP Gun Coy, 1 x SP PzJg Coy)
Führer Begleit Panzergrenadier Regiment
   (HQ Coy, 1 x Pz Fusilier Bn, 1 x (mot) PzGr Bn)
829th Infantry Battalion
   (3 x Rifle Coys, 1 x Hy Coy, 1 x Supply Coy)
Führer Begleit Panzer Battalion
   (HQ 2 x Panther Coys, 1 x Jagdpanther Coy, 1 x PzJg Coy, 1 x StuG Coy, 1 x Supply Coy, 1 x Maint Coy)
Führer Begleit Sturmgeschütz Brigade
   (HQ and HQ Bty, 3 x StuG Btys of 10 StuGs each)
Führer Begleit Artillery Regiment
   (2 x Bns of Bn HQ and HQ Bty, 3 x halftrack Btys, 1 x Supply Bty; FB Flak Bn of 3 Btys)
Führer Begleit Battle School
   (HQ and 3 (mot) Coys
2 x Ambulance Pls
1 x (mot) Med Coy
1 (mot) Maint Coy
2 x Transport Cols

The jaws of the pocket that had been breached were held open by the 2nd Battalion with additional artillery support from artillery units situated in nearby Damm, a suburb of Frankfurt. Part of Kampfgruppe *Langkeit* remained here while the rest was ordered to cross the River Oder. On 3 February Kampfgruppe *Langkeit* was re-formed with new armoured vehicles including new Panther tanks and was renamed the Panzer-Division *Kurmark*.

The division was deployed on the Oder River where the three advancing Soviet fronts had stalled after over-extending their supply lines and it was *Kurmark*'s task to deny the Soviets the high ground east of the Oder which they would need to reconnoitre the whole of the Frankfurt sector. This they did and as a result Soviet attacks in this sector were beaten back. It was not until 16 April that the last Soviet

Right: A Füsilier takes up position ready to fire his *Panzerfaust*—'Armoured Fist'. This close-combat anti-tank weapon was produced in a number of versions with ranges from 30m to 150m and in massive quantities (around eight million of all types from mid-1943 onwards).

offensive was launched, and under the massive Soviet onslaught the units protecting *Kurmark*'s flanks crumbled, resulting in the division being surrounded. All attempts to rescue the trapped division failed.

Ninth Army fell back to the River Spree on 21 April with its units dispersed and unable to fight as a cohesive whole. *Kurmark* was one of these units, by now engaged in heavy combat in the Colpin woods. Halbe was chosen as the point at which a breakout was to be attempted but well positioned pockets of Soviet artillery and armour prevented the planned breakout. The fighting that took place at Halbe was vicious and intense with hand to hand combat as *Kurmark* desperately tried to break the Soviet ring. The division fought in vain as the Soviets had covered every escape route and at Halbe *Kurmark* ceased to exist as a fighting unit. Very few survivors made it out and those that did had to battle their way to the Elbe where there were American positions near Jerichow. Only 30,000 Germans from an entire army made it to the safety of American captivity.

THE FÜHRER BEGLEIT DIVISION

From 1938 a unit from the Wachregiment Berlin was assigned to guard Hitler and did so until the attempt on his life on 20 July 1944. The men for this bodyguard were drawn from the Wachregiment Berlin and then from the *Grossdeutschland* Regiment. They escorted Hitler throughout the Polish campaign and formed the cadre for the Führer-Begleit-Battaillon that was created in October 1939. This followed Hitler throughout the campaign in France. In the aftermath a detachment was sent to Hendaye on the Spanish border as a bodyguard for Hitler during his talks with Spain's General Franco, the remainder staying in Paris to act as official escort for dignitaries. A year later in June 1941, when Hitler moved his HQ to Rastenburg in East Prussia, the Escort Battalion was assigned to guard him there.

To gain some military experience (and credibility) the Kampfgruppe *Nehring* was formed, into which men from the Führer Escort Battalion were rotated for three-month periods of front line duty. The crisis that developed on the Eastern Front during the first Russian winter forced the Kampfgruppe to stay at the front, due to the fact it was about the only well equipped reserve available. As a result of this development the Kampfgruppe was increased in size with the addition of a Panzer company, anti-tank company, motor-cycle and flak platoon, as well as signals and other support units.

Despite this expansion Kampfgruppe *Nehring* never fought as a complete unit under the one command but was split into several small detachments. This resulted in serious losses and it was withdrawn from the front line at the end of March 1942.

In the winter offensive of 1942–43 the Soviets drove through Second Army's sector of the front and among the units sent to hold the line were a heavy weapons company, Panzer company and rifle company of the Führer Escort Battalion. They performed well, and later at Kharkov nearly the whole of Führer Escort Battalion was committed to action with the *Grossdeutschland* Division with a minimal guard being left at the Wolfschanze. The

Below: Sturmgeschütz 40 Ausf G assault guns, most with 'skirts' fitted as a defence against hollow-charged weapons, line-up on a dirt road somewhere on the Eastern Front awaiting orders to advance, December 1943.

Above: The 88mm Panzerschreck close-combat anti-tank weapon was a copy of the American M1 bazooka, first seen in Tunisia. With a range of 150m, it was operated by a two-man team and proved very effective from its introduction in 1943.

Right: Panthers from *Grossdeutschland*—now a Panzer division—are accompanied by a Panzergrenadier carrying an MG 34 during an action on 12 August 1944.

battalion was finally returned to the Wolfschanze in Rastenburg in April 1943 and from it the Führer-Grenadier Division was later raised.

In late 1943 the Soviets opened their third winter offensive. On the Narva Front Army Group North suffered heavy losses and Hitler ordered a Begleit Kampfgruppe to secure the main highway and guard the sea flank from a Soviet seaborne landing. This it did successfully.

On its return to Rastenburg it was suggested that the battalion be expanded to regimental size and kept on permanent standby as a type of 'fire brigade' to be rushed into critical spots at the front. The battalion was subsequently sent to Berchtesgaden and expanded to regimental size with additional manpower from Panzergrenadier Replacement Brigade *Grossdeutschland*. Following the 20 July Bomb Plot Oberst Remer was appointed field commander of the new regiment with Oberst Streve appointed the HQ commander.

On 27 November the Führer Escort Battalion was reinforced to armoured brigade status (Führer-Begleit-Brigade—FBB) and transferred from East Prussia into the Eifel, under Oberst Remer and sent west for the Ardennes Offensive. Stationed on the right flank of the Fifth Panzer Army, it was involved in heavy combat with US forces. On 30 January 1945 the regiment was officially upgraded to divisional status and in February was sent to the Oder Front in company with its sister division the Führer Grenadier Division. Both were involved in very heavy combat against the Soviet Army and the Führer Escort Division was eventually encircled at Spremburg. After a fierce breakout attempt on 21 April 1945 only a handful of survivors remained.

INFANTRY DIVISION/PANZER CORPS *GROSSDEUTSCHLAND*'S RUSSIAN WAR

Date	Corps	Army	Army Group	Area
6.42	Reserve	-	South	Kursk
7.42	XXXXVIII	2nd Army	South	Voronezh
8.42	-	1st Pz Army	A	Manytsch
9.42–11.42	-	9th Army	Centre	Rzhev
12.42	XXIII	9th Army	Centre	Rzhev
1.43	-	9th Army	Centre	Smolensk
2.43	Cramer	-	B	Charkow
3.43–4.43	-	Kempf	South	Charkow
5.43	refreshing	-	-	South Poltava, Karkov
6.43–7.43	XXXXVIII	4th Pz Army	South	Achtyrka, Obojan
8.43	XXIII	2nd Pz Army	Centre	Bryansk
9.43	XXXXVIII	4th Pz Army	South	Krementschug
10.43–12.43	LVII	1st Pz Army	South	Krivoi-Rog
1.44	XXX	6th Army	South	Kirovograd
2.44	LII	8th Army	South	Kirovograd
3.44	XXX	8th Army	South	Kirovograd
4.44–5.44	LVII	8th Army	South Ukraine	Jassy
6.44	refreshing	4th Rumanian Army	South Ukraine	Bacau/Sereth
7.44	reserve	-	South Ukraine	Bacau/Sereth
8.44–9.44	XXXXIX	3rd Pz Army	Centre	Lithuania
10.44–12.44	XXVIII	3rd Pz Army	Centre	Memel
1.45	reorganising	OKH	-	Rastenburg
2.45–3.45	Hermann Goring Corps	4. Army	North	Konigsberg, Pillau
4.45	IX	East Prussia	-	Samland

Above: These men relax in the shade of their shelter quarters (*Zeltbanen*) joined to form a tent supported from the canvas muzzle cover of their Sturmgeschütz.

Left: Flames erupt from a burning T-34 as a self-propelled gun roars past. Based on the PzKpfw 38(t) this is armed with a 75mm PAK 40/3.

Opposite page, above: Painted with in an unusual camouflage scheme, this Marder III passes Hungarian infantry moving forward somewhere in the Upper Dniester and Carpathian area of fighting, May 1944.

Opposite page, below: A hole in the ground, rifle, entrenching tool and field telephone—that is the world of this forward observation post of an artillery battery from *Grossdeutschland* somewhere on the Eastern Front.

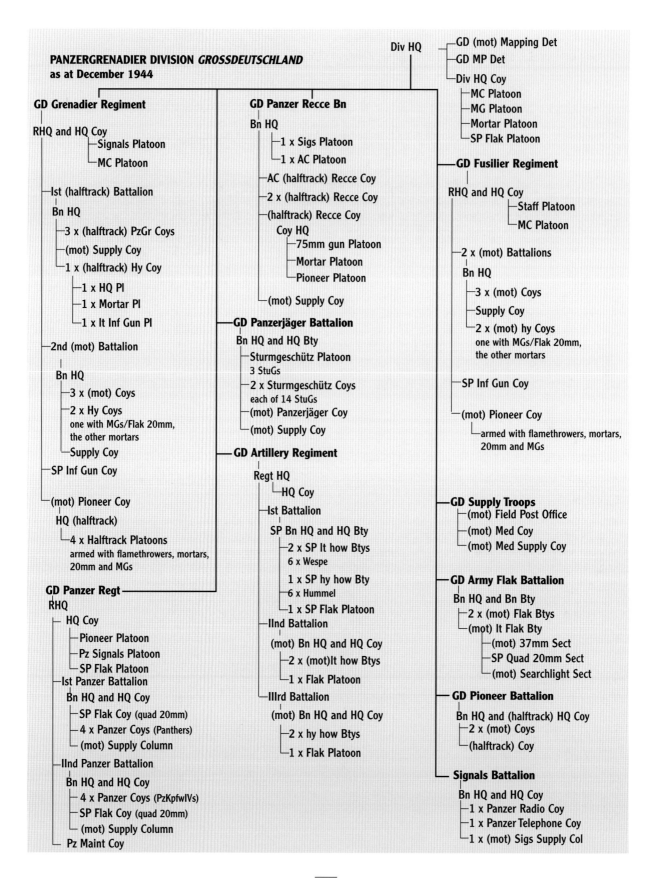

Div HQ
- GD (mot) Mapping Det
- GD MP Det
- Div HQ Coy
  - MC Platoon
  - MG Platoon
  - Mortar Platoon
  - SP Flak Platoon

PANZERGRENADIER DIVISION *GROSSDEUTSCHLAND* as at December 1944

GD Grenadier Regiment

RHQ and HQ Coy
- Signals Platoon
- MC Platoon

Ist (halftrack) Battalion
Bn HQ
- 3 x (halftrack) PzGr Coys
- (mot) Supply Coy
- 1 x (halftrack) Hy Coy
  - 1 x HQ Pl
  - 1 x Mortar Pl
  - 1 x lt Inf Gun Pl

2nd (mot) Battalion

Bn HQ
- 3 x (mot) Coys
- 2 x Hy Coys
  one with MGs/Flak 20mm,
  the other mortars
- Supply Coy

SP Inf Gun Coy

(mot) Pioneer Coy
HQ (halftrack)
- 4 x Halftrack Platoons
  armed with flamethrowers, mortars,
  20mm and MGs

GD Panzer Regt

RHQ
- HQ Coy
  - Pioneer Platoon
  - Pz Signals Platoon
  - SP Flak Platoon
- Ist Panzer Battalion
  Bn HQ and HQ Coy
  - SP Flak Coy (quad 20mm)
  - 4 x Panzer Coys (Panthers)
  - (mot) Supply Column
- IInd Panzer Battalion
  Bn HQ and HQ Coy
  - 4 x Panzer Coys (PzKpfwIVs)
  - SP Flak Coy (quad 20mm)
  - (mot) Supply Column
- Pz Maint Coy

GD Panzer Recce Bn

Bn HQ
- 1 x Sigs Platoon
- 1 x AC Platoon
- AC (halftrack) Recce Coy
- 2 x (halftrack) Recce Coy
- (halftrack) Recce Coy
  Coy HQ
  - 75mm gun Platoon
  - Mortar Platoon
  - Pioneer Platoon
- (mot) Supply Coy

GD Panzerjäger Battalion

Bn HQ and HQ Bty
- Sturmgeschütz Platoon
  3 StuGs
- 2 x Sturmgeschütz Coys
  each of 14 StuGs
- (mot) Panzerjäger Coy
- (mot) Supply Coy

GD Artillery Regiment

Regt HQ
- HQ Coy
- Ist Battalion
  SP Bn HQ and HQ Bty
  - 2 x SP lt how Btys
    6 x Wespe
  - 1 x SP hy how Bty
    6 x Hummel
  - 1 x SP Flak Platoon
- IInd Battalion
  (mot) Bn HQ and HQ Coy
  - 2 x (mot)lt how Btys
  - 1 x Flak Platoon
- IIIrd Battalion
  (mot) Bn HQ and HQ Coy
  - 2 x hy how Btys
  - 1 x Flak Platoon

GD Fusilier Regiment

RHQ and HQ Coy
- Staff Platoon
- MC Platoon

2 x (mot) Battalions
Bn HQ
- 3 x (mot) Coys
- Supply Coy
- 2 x (mot) hy Coys
  one with MGs/Flak 20mm,
  the other mortars

SP Inf Gun Coy

(mot) Pioneer Coy
- armed with flamethrowers, mortars,
  20mm and MGs

GD Supply Troops
- (mot) Field Post Office
- (mot) Med Coy
- (mot) Med Supply Coy

GD Army Flak Battalion

Bn HQ and Bn Bty
- 2 x (mot) Flak Btys
- (mot) lt Flak Bty
  - (mot) 37mm Sect
  - SP Quad 20mm Sect
  - (mot) Searchlight Sect

GD Pioneer Battalion

Bn HQ and (halftrack) HQ Coy
- 2 x (mot) Coys
- (halftrack) Coy

Signals Battalion

Bn HQ and HQ Coy
- 1 x Panzer Radio Coy
- 1 x Panzer Telephone Coy
- 1 x (mot) Sigs Supply Col

HISTORY OF PANZER *GROSSDEUTSCHLAND* ERSATZ (REPLACEMENT) BRIGADE

1 June 1942	Formed as GD's training unit with constituent elements GD (mot) Infantry Ersatz Regt and GD Artillery Ersatz Bn.
10 Feb 1943	Fast Troop Training Battalion included (ceases end 1943).
Feb 1945	Sees action near Forst.
10 Mar 1945	Used to restore Brandenburg PzGdr Division.
Spring 1945	Reformed as PzGdr Ersatz und Ausbildungs Brigade GD.
4 Apr 1945	Reorganised on paper to include:

GD Panzer Ausbildungs Battalion, GD Panzergrenadier Ausbildungs Regiment (3 x Abteilungen), GD Officer Candidate School, GD Panzer Artillery Ausbildungs Battalion, GD Panzer Pioneer Ausbildungs Battalion (2 x Coys), GD Panzer Signals Ausbildungs Battalion (1 x Coy), 20th Panzer Ausbildungs Battalion. Taken into 15th PzGdr Division, it surrendered to the British at the end of the war.

OFFICIAL PERSONNEL AND EQUIPMENT ESTABLISHMENT OF A TYPE 1944 PANZERGRENADIER DIVISION
as at 1 August 1944

Personnel

	Officers	Other Ranks		Officers	Other Ranks
Division HQ	23	168	Artillery Regiment	48	1,522
2 PzGr Regiments total of	150	6,064	Army Flak Battalion	18	617
(inc 3 x PzGr Bn each of	20	848)	(mot) Pioneer Battalion	17	816
Panzer Battalion	21	581	(mot) Signals Battalion	13	414
SP Panzerjäger Battalion	17	458	Replacement Battalion	17	956
Panzer Recce Battalion	23	982	Others (Medical, Admin, etc)	23	1,039
			TOTAL	370	13,617

Equipment

	HMGs	LMGs	75mm Pak40	80mm mortar	120mm mortar	20mm flak	150mm hy gun	flame-thrower	20mm SP quad
Division HQ	0	4	0	0	0	0	0	0	0
2 Panzergrenadier Regiments total of	28	182	6	16	24	36	8	36	0
(inc 3 x PzGr Bn each of	12	66	0	6	12	18	0	0	0
Panzer Battalion	0	0	0	0	0	0	0	0	3
SP Panzerjäger Battalion	0	21	12	0	0	0	0	0	0
Panzer Recce Battalion	12	48	0	12	0	0	0	0	0
Artillery Regiment	0	44	0	0	0	0	0	0	0
Army Flak Battalion	0	10	0	6	0	10	0	0	0
(mot) Pioneer Battalion	0	57	0	6	0	0	0	0	0
(mot) Signals Battalion	0	13	0	0	0	0	0	0	0
Replacement Battalion	12	68	1	6	2	1	0	2	0
Others (Medical, Admin, etc)	0	14	0	0	0	0	0	0	0
TOTAL	52	461	19	46	26	47	8	38	3

	PzBef WglV	AC	StuG 75mm	PzJgIV 75mm	20mm	105mm leFH	150mm sFH	100mm gun	88mm gun	37mm flak	20mm SP
Panzer Battalion	3	4	42	0	0	0	0	0	0	0	0
SP Panzerjäger Battalion	0	0	0	31	0	0	0	0	0	0	0
Panzer Recce Battalion	0	17 hy*	0	0	0	0	0	0	0	0	0
Artillery Regiment	0	0	0	0	9	36	12	6	0	0	0
Army Flak Battalion	0	0	0	0	6	0	0	0	8	9	3
Replacement Battalion	0	0	0	0	0	1	0	0	0	0	0
TOTAL	3	21	42	31	15	37	12	6	8	9	3

*or 20 light. Armament 16 LMGs, 13 20mm, 3 75mm guns.

INSIGNIA & MARKINGS

Like all German units, *Grossdeutschland* used extensive vehicle markings and uniform insignia to distinguish it on the battlefield. There was, of course, great variety in the type of personal equipment with which the individual soldier might be issued, but like all armies a large degree of uniformity existed.

GROSSDEUTSCHLAND INSIGNIA

The German Army had a complex system of uniform colouring that was used to distinguish soldiers from different types of units. This colouring was used as piping and edging or *Waffenfarbe* (arm of service colours) on the uniform and, as the name suggests, was determined by the soldier's arm of service. Infantrymen wore white *Waffenfarbe*, and engineers wore black. Various devices were used along with the *Waffenfarbe* to distinguish the individual unit to which the soldier belonged. *Grossdeutschland* wore white *Waffenfarbe* with an entwined 'GD'.

The German Army also had specialist badges, which were worn by soldiers under the rank of Leutnant. The badges were either worn on the lower right, upper left, or lower left sleeve of the tunic. Such badges were awarded for having suffered battle injuries, destroyed enemy tanks or aircraft, sniping successes and the like.

Because of the great diversity of units that were attached to GD, it is impossible to describe in detail each one of the uniform styles. However, among the infantrymen there were some standard features. The most distinctive part of *Grossdeutschland* insignia was a cuff band, worn on the right arm below the elbow, in contrast to the SS formations which wore their cuffbands on the left.

Upon its redesignation as a regiment in 1937 the main source unit, the Wachtruppe Berlin, was issued with a Gothic style 'W' patch that was worn on the epaulettes and shoulder patches. When the infantry training battalion at Döberitz, the other source unit, was expanded the same year, its members added a Gothic 'L' to their epaulettes.

In the German Army, the issue of a cuff band traditionally denoted status as an elite unit and in August 1940 a black cuff title bearing the legend '*Inf.-Reg Großdeutschland*' was issued to the unit. Later, in November, the Führer Escort Battalion, which was formed from *Grossdeutschland*, received its own cuff band. GD's own cuff band changed on a number of occasions

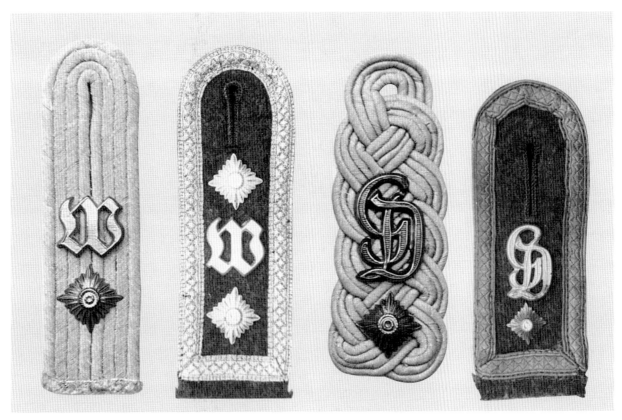

Above: An unnamed Oberleutnant showing the *Grossdeutschland* 'GD' on his shoulder strap and the collar *Litzen* denoting an assault artillery unit.

Right: Eastern Front action from the pages of *Signal*, the Wehrmacht's magazine that was published fortnightly from April 1940 to March 1945.

during the war. Thus, in October 1940 its colour as changed to green, and the legend was simplified to '*Großdeutschland*'. Subsequently, although the legend remained the same, the style and size of the type was changed another four times.

The Führer-Begleit-Bataillon, formed from the ranks of the regiment, was issued on 15 January with an extra cuffband, inscribed with the legend in Gothic German type 'Führer-Hauptquartier' (headquarters) to be worn below the GD band.

UNIFORMS

There now follows a description of what a typical soldier of the Panzer-Füsilier-Regiment would have worn during the 1944–45 period, and a description of the Sturmartillerie uniform from the same period.

The Panzer-Füsilier of 1944–45 would typically be dressed in one of two uniform styles. The first was the standard German Army M43 Tunic with M42 or M43 trousers. The second would be the assault artillery (Sturmartillerie) uniform. This uniform was issued to GD's SPW mounted battalions in 1944.

The M43 Uniform

The M43 uniform tunic was a rationalisation of the M36 design, which had a plain collar, flat, unpleated, unpointed chest pockets and unpointed bellows skirt pockets. At the beginning of the war this was made predominantly from wool, but cellulose was increasingly used over the war years, and as a result the M43 was more cellulose than wool. The lining was made from rayon. As a result of this degradation in fabric quality the tunic now had to be fastened with six buttons. In addition to displaying the *Litzen* (the collar patches that identified rank and arm of service), the collar could also display the dull grey non-commissioned officer's *Tresse* (braid) worn by holders of ranks from Unteroffizier to Hauptfeldwebel. The national emblem of an eagle clutching a Swastika was placed above the right breast pocket, and the divisional cuff band sewn 19cm above the cuff on the right sleeve. The field-grey shoulder straps were piped in white, and the shoulder strap was embroidered with the famous entwined GD monogram. Senior NCOs and officers wore metal versions of this emblem in grey and gilt metal respectively. NCOs' shoulder straps were also edged with the *Tresse* mentioned earlier.

The Sturmartillerie Uniform

In 1944 the armoured battalions of the *Grossdeutschland* infantry regiments (1. Battaillon Panzer-Grenadier-Regiment GD and 1. Battaillon, Panzer-Füsilier-Regiment GD) were issued the Sturmartillerie uniform (though only the first battalions of the motorised infantry regiments were equipped with SPWs). The Sturmartillerie uniform was the same as the Army's black Panzer uniform but in a field grey cloth. The blouson-style jacket was cut at the waist and fastened with a row of buttons arranged vertically on the right hand side. The collar was large and worn open but could be fastened at the neck with a hook and eye. The trousers were tapered toward the ankles giving a bloused effect over the top of the boot. The trousers had an integral belt and front pockets with pocket flaps. The standard GD insignia were worn on this uniform, although the collar Litzen was a standard Litzen over a lozenge shaped patch of field grey wool piped in white, the infantry Waffenfarbe. Officers wore their normal collar insignia attached directly to the collar. Standard white piped shoulder boards were worn with this uniform.

Underclothes

Under the tunic the Panzer fusilier would wear a shirt of either a grey jersey material, or a green or grey cotton, with and without pockets, grey woollen socks or the German copy of the Russian footwraps. Those with experience of conditions on the Eastern Front usually wore footwraps, for extra warmth.

Footwear

Early pictures of *Grossdeutschland* show the troops shod in the familiar German marching boot, but by 1944-45 leather shortages meant that the boot been much reduced in height, and most new recruits were issued with a new style ankle boot. The German Army had trialed the ankle boot in 1935 and re-introduced it in 1942. The style varied according to the manufacturer. Some were all eyeholes, others eyeholes and hooks, some were rough side out on the upper, others were smooth side out all over. In 1944–45 they were supplied in their natural colour, brown.

If they were worn with the M42/M43 trousers, the soldier would probably tuck the ends of the trousers into standard issue gaiters. These were made of heavy canvas and had two buckles and straps to fasten them around the ankles. The gaiters provided some ankle support and also prevented stones and twigs getting into the boots. If worn with the Sturmartillerie uniform then the trousers were probably tucked straight into the boots or into rolled over socks.

In the bitterly cold Russian winters, other types of lined boots found favour with those that could get them.

Headwear

Although, the Panzer-Füsilier in 1944–45 was issued with both the M42 pattern *Stahlhelm* (steel helmet) or the M43 pattern *Einheitsfeldmütze* (field cap), pictures from this period indicate that the latter was more commonly worn.

The M42 helmet was a version of the M35 simplified for quicker production by leaving the rim uncrimped and by casting the ventilation holes directly into the

Below: German infantry move out of their fixed positions during the fighting around Kharkov, 1 June 1942. Note ammunition boxes, MG 34 and other personal equipment.

helmet shell itself. The M43 cap was the standardised field head gear for Army troops, and replaced the previous M38, M40 and M42 pattern caps in production. It was made from field grey wool and featured a long peak, over which the national insignia was stitched. Officers' caps had silver piping to the crown seam, and sometimes this was also placed onto the scallop of the turn up.

In addition the extreme cold of the Russian winter led to a profusion of unofficial fur, fur-trimmed or fur-lined, and wool hats, some of which were donated by the German public after a formal request was made by the Propaganda Ministry.

Other Clothing

Although winter clothing was always in short supply on the Eastern Front, *Grossdeutschland*'s status as an elite unit meant that it got the best of the equipment. It was one of the first units to receive the mouse grey and white (reversible) winter parka issued in the winter of 1942–43, and its men were also issued with numerous other camouflage smocks and snow suits. Another item that was commonly worn over the battledress was the camouflage shelter quarter (see below). Officers overcoats varied greatly from the standard issue field grey type, to the heavy sheepskin-lined item favoured by Generalleutnant Hoernlein.

FIELD EQUIPMENT

Karabiner 98 (K-98)

Introduced in 1898, this rifle (*Gewehr*) was the standard infantry weapon of all German forces. The Kar 98k was introduced in 1935. This weapon, despite plans to replace it with weapons of greater firepower and lower production costs, remained the primary infantry weapon for the entire conflict.

Gewehr/Karabiner 43 (G-43/K-43)

The need for a weapon with greater firepower was recognised early in the war. The unsuccessful G-41, with its complicated muzzle gas cap system was scrapped after delivery of approximately 70,000 rifles, and after examination of captured Russian auto-loaders, the gas system of the Tokarev (SVT40) was incorporated into a new rifle, while retaining the Mauser G-41 extraction system. The new rifle was introduced into service on 30 April 1943. Approximately 350,000 were delivered by 1945.

Maschinen-Pistole 40 (MP-40)

The MP-40 was an improved version of the MP-38 sub-machine gun, intended for use by paratroops and by armoured vehicle crews. It was intended for simple mass construction. Total production was more than a million guns in 1940–44.

Stick Grenade Model 39

The M39 stick grenade was the standard hand grenade of the German Army throughout the war. The grenade consisted of a thin, metal, explosive filled,

Above: 'Only seconds before the attack, a smokescreen already blinds the enemy pocket of resistance. An assault leader glances behind him before launching himself from cover into the open, August 1943.' So reads the original caption. Certainly the soldier is ready for action; he's left his pack and other weighty equipment behind, has used some foliage to disguise the outline of his helmet and is armed with an MP40 machine-pistol.

cylindrical head that was screwed onto a hollow wooden handle. A friction pull igniter activated the timed fuse when a cord (ending in a porcelain ball) was pulled. The grenade was kept in the 'safe' position by use of a screw off end cap on the wooden handle, which kept the cord and porcelain ball safely in the wooden handle. The fuse time was 4–5 seconds.

Bayonet, Frog and Scabbard
The bayonet frog was used to carry the scabbard on the cartridge belt. It was constructed of leather and came in two styles: mounted and dismounted. The mounted version had a leather tab that would secure the grip of the bayonet to the frog. The bayonet was the final pattern 84/98 Mauser bayonet. The handle was constructed either of wood or Bakelite plastic. The scabbard was made of stamped metal and had a ball on the tip to prevent the scabbard from getting caught on clothing.

Cartridge Belt and Buckle
The leather cartridge belt had a clasp attached to it to be secured at the buckle. The buckle was constructed either of aluminum or steel. The buckle was either unfinished or painted green, with an eagle to denote a Wehrmacht unit.

Cartridge Belt Suspenders
In 1939 testing began on externally worn cartridge belt suspenders. By taking the straps from the Model 1934 field pack and replacing the sewn-on leather pack attachment tabs with D-rings, the external cartridge belt suspenders were created. By late 1940 the new suspenders were in use by the infantry. By 1943 the transition from internal to external suspenders was complete. The suspenders were

Below: Another *Signal* photograph, showing German infantry in 1943. Note colour of uniforms and webbing, and Iron Cross on front man.

produced in two different styles: the dismounted and the mounted. The foot soldier would normally be issued the heavier, dismounted style. The dismounted is identified by the wider shoulder straps, heavier construction, D-ring attachments on the rear of the shoulder harness, and attached lower pack straps which were used for securing the bottom of any attached pack.

Combat Assault Pack
The combat assault pack or A-frame was constructed of a canvas web shaped like an A. This pack was designed to carry essential equipment into action. The A-frame was designed to be used specifically with the dismounted style of leather cartridge-belt suspender. When used, the pack provided places for carrying the shelter quarter, the mess kit, the greatcoat and/or blanket. These items were strapped to the pack with black leather straps.

Model 1938 Gasmask and Canister
The German soldier was issued the Model 1938 gasmask, or GM38. The GM38 was made of synthetic rubber and was fitted with either the FE37, FE41, or FE42 filter elements, which screwed into the snout of the mask. The GM38 had two vision ports. Besides the five elastic straps used to secure the mask to the face, there was a long canvas web strap used to suspend the GM38 around the neck. The fluted metal canister, with a spring loaded lid catch, contained the mask when it was not in use. A small box, on the inside of the lid of the canister, contained two pairs of replacement eyelet covers. A cleaning cloth was also housed in the canister.

Entrenching Tool
The entrenching tool was manufactured in two versions: folding and non-folding. The non-folding type was from a WWI design and had a square blade. The folding tool was designed as a replacement for the older version and began to appear in early 1940. The folding blade was pointed and could be adjusted by means of a Bakelite nut to open at a 90° or 180° angle for digging in. Both versions were stored in carriers suspended from the cartridge belt. The e-tool was also used as a close combat weapon.

Above: The German advance into Russia in 1941 was at such a rate that the infantry were hard-pressed to complete the massive encircling operations. In spite of the 'motorised' nature of the Panzergrenadier, all too often he had to rely on his own two feet to get him into and out of battle. Note the personal equipment—particularly the marching boots: they would be in short supply as the war progressed.

Zeltbahn

The *Zeltbahn* (shelter quarter) or rain poncho, was used both for inclement weather protection and/or camouflage. Made in the shape of a triangle, it had 62 buttons. When four were buttoned together, it produced a 'four-man tent' in pyramid shape, though 'four-man' meant that it was only large enough for three soldiers to squeeze inside; the fourth man was expected to stand sentry duty. The intrepid German soldier found a variety of additional uses for this item. It could be used to form a lean-to shelter or carry a wounded comrade to the aid station, or, as mentioned above, could be an item of clothing. The camouflage pattern seen on the poncho was known as 'splinter' type. See photograph on page 157 for an example of the use of the *Zeltbahn*.

Breadbag Model 1931

The breadbag was carried by every German foot soldier. This satchel was used for carrying a soldier's rations and small personal items: butterdish, fork-spoon, tablet-fuel stove, individual weapon cleaning kit, field cap, dust goggles, extra matches, tobacco, playing cards, etc. The outside of the bag flap could be used for securing the mess tin and canteen.

Below: German grenadiers, wearing greatcoats and carrying rifles, were carried on the back of tanks and self-propelled assault guns towards the enemy.

Mess Kit Model 1931

A mess kit was carried by every German foot soldier. The kit was constructed of two pieces of painted aluminium, which were designed to fit tightly together to form a single container. The lower bowl portion was used for soups and stews, while the upper plate portion was for more solid fare. The mess kit sections, when clamped together, could be used to transport rations for future consumption. Both pieces could be used for cooking, but this quickly destroyed the flat, field-grey or olive drab painted finish.

Canteen and Cup Model 1931

The canteen Model 1931 carried by every German foot soldier, had a capacity of about one litre. The bottle was carried in a brown felt cover that was snapped around it. The drinking cup was made of pressed aluminium, which was painted black and secured to the canteen by a leather strap. The whole canteen was then secured to the breadbag for carrying in the field.

Butterdish

The butterdish or fat container was constructed of Bakelite plastic that was made of two pieces and screwed together. Part of a soldier's daily ration was fat such as butter, margarine or lard. These fats were spread on the bread ration. The butterdish was normally carried in the breadbag.

Soldbuch

The Soldbuch or soldier's pay book was his identity package. This book was on his person at all times. Official entries included a photo i.d. and a record of such things as place of birth, name, equipment numbers, pay records, leave entitlement and so on. Most soldiers also used the Soldbuch to carry money, photos, letters from family, wives, girlfriends, etc.

Identification Disc

As in most armies every foot soldier was issued an i.d. disc, and was required to wear it at all times. The oval zinc i.d. disc was divided in half by perforated slots, and had holes for a cord so that it could be worn about the neck. The information on the disc consisted of the soldier's personnel roster number that was also recorded in his *Soldbuch*, the unit he was assigned to, and his blood type. This was recorded identically on the other half of the disc. In case of death, the disc was broken in half. The portion with the cord stayed on the body for later identification and the other half went to his family with his personal effects.

GROSSDEUTSCHLAND VEHICLE MARKINGS

In September, 1940, during the unit's organisation as a motorised infantry regiment and at the suggestion of the regimental commander Oberst Stockhausen, the familiar white *Stahlhelm* (steel helmet) symbol was chosen to identify regimental vehicles. This remained as the unit insignia for the duration of the war, although it was used in a wide diversity of combinations.

Vehicles carried divisional, tactical, unit and individual markings on the rear. In May 1940 vehicles of the four battalions were distinguished by a square, circle, triangle, or rhombus, over which was painted an identical but smaller shape of contrasting colours, and inside that the divisional Stahlhelm insignia. Command

Above: The battered *Soldbuch* of a German infantryman who served on the Eastern Front.

Below: The white helmet that signifies Grossdeutschland is just visible on the back of this eight-wheeled armoured car. Note frame aerial.

Above: Crew of an Sd Kfz 251 armoured personnel carrier eat from their mess tins without leaving their vehicle. Note the divisional sign of *Grossdeutschland* —the white helmet—painted on the front engine cowling; 14 September 1943.

Below and Right: Two more *Signal* views of *Panzers* in Russia. From 1942 *Grossdeutschland* although it was an infantry division, had tank battalions. By 1944 it was the Army's most powerful infantry unit

vehicles were distinguished by a three-colour pennant, with the 'GD' legend on the white central portion. As additional units were assigned to GD they adopted their own markings. For example, the *Kradschützen* (motorcycle battalion) used a cross bounded by a circle, in addition to the Stahlhelm

Vehicles carried further distinguishing insignia on the front mudguard or the front wing, which in mid-1944 were as follows:

Headquarters (Stab)—GD Pennant on rhombus.

HQ Panzer Regiment—plain square pennant on rhombus.

1st, 2nd, 3rd Battalions Panzer Regiment—plain triangular pennant on rhombus.

HQ Armoured Grenadier Infantry—plain square pennant on SPW symbol.

1st, 2nd, 3rd Armoured Grenadier Infantry battalions—triangular pennant flanked by two circles (to represent wheels of a truck).

HQ Armoured Fusilier Infantry—dark square pennant on SPW symbol.

1st, 2nd, 3rd Armoured Fusilier Infantry battalions—triangular dark pennant flanked by two circles.

Panzer Reconnaissance Detachment (Aufklärungs-Abteilung)—triangular pennant on rhombus masted by smaller pennant.

Flak Abteilung—plain triangular pennant on small circle. Upward pointing arrow on pennant shaft.

HQ Panzer Artillery Regiment—plain square pennant on rhombus. Two vertical lines flank the pennant shaft.

1st Panzer Artillery Regiment—plain triangular pennant on oval. Two vertical lines flank the pennant shaft.

2nd, 3rd, 4th Panzer Artillery Regiments—plain triangular pennant on rhombus. Two vertical lines flank the pennant shaft.

Sturmgeschütz Brigade—plain triangular pennant with border on rhombus. Upward pointing arrow on pennant shaft.

Panzer Engineer Battalion—plain triangular pennant on rhombus. Two upward pointing arrows on top of the pennant shaft.

Panzer Signals Detachment (*Nachrichten Abteilung*)—plain triangular pennant on rhombus. Single upward pointing arrow on top of the pennant shaft.

Divisions Nachstub Truppe—plain triangular pennant flanked by two circles, two small horizontal lines on pennant shaft.

Replacement Battalion—plain triangular pennant.

PEOPLE

Right: Detachment Commander Major Possl was awarded the Knight's Cross of the Iron Cross in May 1943.

Grossdeutschland's performance in combat and its high press profile ensured that many of its soldiers became household names in wartime Germany. The unit also won a significant numbers of the Ritterkreuz (the Knight's Cross to the Iron Cross) for gallantry. Below are listed the Ritterkreuzträger of the *Grossdeutschland* Panzer Corps, with biographies of some of the most significant personalities.

GROSSDEUTSCHLAND RITTERKREUZTRÄGER

Friedrich Anding	Hans Hindelang	Oldwig Natzmer	Georg Stork
Hans-Dieter Basse	Walter Hoernlein	Werner Neumeyer	Hyazinth Strachwitz Gross
Helmut Beck-Broichitter	Max Holm	Heinrich Nuhn	Zauche und Camminetz
Heinz Bergmann	Ernst-Albrecht Huckel	? Paul	Hans Hermann Sturm
Martin Bielig	Erich Kahsnitz	Otto Pfau	Nepomuk Stuzle
Carl-Ludwig Blumenthal	Franz Kapsreiter	Fritz Plickat	Hans Thiessan
Hans Bock	Bernhard Kelmz	Wilhelm Pohlmann	Gotfried Tornau
Georg Bohnk	Willi Kessel	Leopold Poschusta	Horst Usedom
Max Bohrendt	Rudi Kirsten	Walther Possl	Gustav Walle
Heinz Wittchow Brese-Winiary	Hans Klemm	Josef Rampel	Horst Warschnaur
Wilhelm Czorny	Heinrich Klemt	Hans Friedrich Graf zu Rantzau	Rudolf Watjen
Diddens Diddo	Ludwig Kohlhaas	Adam Reidmuller	Wilhelm Wegner
Maxemilian Fabich	Gerhard Konopka	Hans Roger	Walther Wietersheim
Gunther Famula	Gerhard Krieg	Emil Rossman	
Franz Fischer	Harold Kriegk	Hans Siegfried Graf Rotkirch	
Edmund Francois	Willi Langkiet	und Trach	
Adolf Frankl	Rudolf Larsen	Hans Sachs	
Peter Frantz	Ernst G. Lehnhoff	Kurt Scheumann	
Eugen Garski	Hans Lex	Hugo Schimmel	
Kurt Gehrke	Siegfried Leyck	E. Schmidt	
Alfred Greim	Karl Lorenz	Georg Schnappauf	
Wilhelm Griesberg	Heinz Maaz	Hans-Wolfgang Schone	
Karl Hanert	Helmut Mader	Erich Schroedter	
Wolfgang Heesemann	Hanns Magold	Rudolf Schwarzrock	
Willi Heinrich	Hasso-Eckard Manteuffel	Clemens Sommer	
Herbert Hensel	Siegmund Matheja	Ruprecht Sommer	
Josef Herbst	Leonhard Mollendorf	Helmuth Spaeter	

OBERST HEINZ WITTCHOW VON BRESE-WINIARY

Born on 13 January 1914 in Dresden, Brese-Winiary won his Knight's Cross and his Oakleaves to the Knight's Cross while commander of 1./PzGr Regiment 108. He joined GD later in the war, being promoted to Oberst whilst serving with *Grossdeutschland* Panzer Corps.

Brese-Winiary joined the German Army in April 1934 as a member of Infantry Regiment 10 in Dresden and in May 1936 was promoted to the rank of Leutnant. Over the next few years he served as a company officer and battalion signals officer with the 10th Infantry. In May 1939 he was again promoted this time to the rank of Oberleutnant and became a battalion adjutant. On 24 October 1939 he was awarded the Iron Cross 2nd Class. He was awarded the Iron Cross 1st Class on 24 June 1940 whilst serving in France, and on 31 October 1940 he was awarded the Infantry Assault Badge. He then went on to serve in Russia and, as a survivor of the terrible winter of 1941–42, was awarded the Eastern Front Medal. He was also wounded during 1941 while serving in Russia and received the Wound Badge in Black and in December 1941 received the German Cross in Gold.

On 1 March 1942 he was promoted to the rank of Hauptmann and became company commander of the 6th Company IR10. He subsequently served as commander of 2nd Battalion, Panzer-Grenadier-Regiment 108 and 2nd Battalion, Panzer-Grenadier-Regiment 103 and from 14 December 1942 through to 22 February 1943 was commander of Kampfgruppe *Brese*, involved in combat near Stalingrad. During this time he was wounded again and awarded the Wound Badge in both Silver and Gold. In April 1943 he was promoted to the rank of Major and on 15 May 1943 he was awarded the Ritterkreuz. He later on became regimental commander of Panzer-Grenadier-Regiment 108 and fought at the Cherkassy Pocket where he earned the Oakleaves to the Ritterkreuz. He was awarded the Close Combat Clasp on 23 March 1944 and on 1 April 1944 he was promoted to the rank of Oberstleutnant. Finally, on 1 September 1944 he was promoted to Oberst.

As of 3 September 1944 until the end of the war (he surrendered to the Soviets on 18 February 1945) his assignment was commander of Panzer-Füsilier-Regiment *Grossdeutschland* in the *Grossdeutschland* Division.

Brese-Winiary died in 1991.

Below: On 5 April 1943 Hauptmann Magold from the Sturmgeschütz-Abteilung Grossdeutschland received the Knight's Cross of the Iron Cross. During the period from 7 to 18 March 1943, his battery destroyed 26 Soviet tanks and 50 anti-tank weapons around Kharkov.

HERBERT KARL 'HANS' MAGOLD

Born on 16 November 1918, in Unterssfeld, Bad Königshofen im Grabfeld, Bavaria, Magold joined the German Army in 1937 and served in the Polish French and Balkans campaigns. He took part in the invasion of Russia and went on to command 5th Battalion Panzer Regiment 74 in 1942. He was wounded in August 1942 and was sent back to Germany. On his return he commanded 1st Sturmgeschütz Abteilung *Grossdeutschland* in February 1943 in which role he took part in the battles around Kharkov. A short while afterwards during an engagement with Soviet armour he personally accounted for the destruction of five T-34s for which he was awarded the

Ritterkreuz. He was killed in action on 15 September 1944, during the defensive battles at Luzagora near the Dukla Pass in Poland.

HASSO-ECKARD VON MANTEUFFEL

Born on 14 January 1897 in Potsdam, Hasso-Eckard Manteuffel was a career soldier. He joined the Cadet Academy Berlin-Lichterfelde in 1911 at the age of 14 and went on to serve in France with the 3rd Brandenburg Hussar Regiment *Ziethen* as a Leutnant. In October 1916 he transferred with the 5th Squadron to the 6th (Prussian) Infantry Division and at the end of the war was engaged in protecting the Rhine bridges to safeguard the retreat of the field Army. Post-war he served in Freikorps *Oven* in Berlin and was subsequently a squadron commander and adjutant in the 3rd Cavalry Regiment in the 100,000 man Reichswehr. In February 1930 he was promoted Oberleutnant and made chief of the technical squadron of his regiment, and in 1932 was appointed a squadron commander in the 17th Cavalry Regiment. Promoted Hauptmann der Kavallerie in April 1934, in October of that year he transferred to the 2nd Motorcycle Rifle Battalion of the rapidly expanding Wehrmacht and became staff major and training officer of all cadet officers of 2nd Panzer Division 1936–37.

From 25 February 1937 Manteuffel was official adviser to the Inspectorate of Panzer Troops under Guderian at OKH and, subsequently, head of the directing staff at Panzer Troops School II at Berlin-Krampnitz. He was promoted Major in September 1939, Oberstleutnant in July 1941, and Oberst in October 1941, commanding Schützen-Regiment 2 and then 6. On 23 November 1941, during the 7th Panzer Division's final attack towards Moscow Manteuffel's Schützen-Regiment took Klin. By 27 November the area 2½ miles north-west of the bridge at Jakhroma over the Moscow–Volga canal was occupied. Early on 28 November Manteuffel's battle group began an attack in this sector, with the further aim of crossing the canal. They achieved both objectives. On 31 December 1941 Oberst Manteuffel was awarded the Knight's Cross for this operation, to accompany the Iron Cross 1st Class he had won in May 1917.

After being given brief command of Division *Manteuffel* in North Africa (7 February 1943–31 March 1943) he launched a very successful counter-attack in the Tunis area cutting Allied lines. He then led the 7th Panzer Division, being promoted Generalmajor in May 1943 and winning Oakleaves to his Knight's Cross in November that year. He became commander of Panzer-Grenadier-Division *Grossdeutschland* at the end of January 1944, being promoted Generalleutnant.

In 1944 he was awarded Oak Leaves with Swords to the Knight's Cross, before being promoted further in September—to the command of the Fifth Panzer Army as a General der Panzertruppen. This unit won impressive victories during the

Above: On 8 May 1944 a communiqué from the German High Command announced that Generalleutnant von Manteuffel, commander of Panzer Division *Grossdeutschland*, had been awarded the addition of the Oak Leaves with Swords to his Knight's Cross.

Right: Gerhard Konopka, an officer in the *Reichsarbeitedienst* (German Labour Service) and an Oberleutnant der Reserve serving with *Grossdeutschland*, received his Knight's Cross in October 1943. He is seen here wearing his RAD uniform complete with his other military awards (including four *Panzervernichtungsabzeichen* (tank destruction badges) surrounded by admiring young members of the RAD.

Centre right: On 12 November 1942, at the invitation of Dr. Joseph Goebbels, Reichsminister for Propaganda, representatives of the German troops engaged in fighting around Rshev were received in his Berlin ministry. Here he is seen admiring a painting and a captured Cossack sword presented to him by these visiting troops. Standing to his right is Oberleutant Gerhard Konopka and directly behind him Generalleutnant von Hase, Commandant (*Stadtkommandant*) of Berlin.

Below right. Knight's Cross holder, Major Kriegk, commander of the Panzergrenadier Regiment *Grossdeutschland* (wearing bandage), with his adjutant on 14 July 1944.

Below: Hauptmann Hans Lex, Knight's Cross holder and company commander in Panzer Regiment *Grossdeutschland*, 9 October 1943.

Above left: Oberst Lorenz, Commander of the Panzergrenadier Regiment *Grossdeutschland*, offers a drink from his waterbottle to one of his grenadiers, 30 May 1944.

Left: Oberst Graf Strachwitz (right), commander of one of the division's tank regiments, here conferring with one of his tank commanders. Note the stand-off turret armour on the PzKpfw IV behind him.

Above: Oberst Lorenz (wearing cap), commander of Panzergrenadier Regiment *Grossdeutschland*, in conversation with Oberleutnant Konopka. Both are *Ritterkreuzträger*.

Below: The CO of Panzergrenadier Division *Grossdeutschland*, Generalleutnant Hoernlein, in conversation with Oberst Graf Strachwitz (left) on 15 October 1943. Note Strachwitz's cuff title.

Above: Generalmajor Hoernlein standing on his command vehicle observing the effect of a Stuka attack against Soviet positions, August 1942.

Battle of Bulge and almost succeeded in breaking the Allied defence lines. After this battle, Manteuffel became the commander of Third Panzer Army, part of Army Group Weichsel (Vistula), which tried to slow down the Soviet advance on Berlin. On 3 May 1945 he surrendered to the Western allies.

In 1953–57 Manteuffel was a member of the Bundestag and represented the Free Democratic Party. In 1959 he was charged with ordering a 19-year old to be shot for desertion in 1944 and was sentenced to 18 months in prison but was released after serving four months. He died on 24 September 1978 in Reith in Alpbachtal, Austria.

ERNST-OTTO REMER

Born in 1912 Remer was commander of the *Grossdeutschland* Battalion in Berlin at the time of the 20 July 1944 Bomb Plot. Initially he carried out the orders of Oberst Claus Stauffenberg to deploy his *Grossdeutschland* Battalion in and around Berlin's government quarter, but swiftly defected to the side of the regime after speaking to Reich Propaganda Minister Joseph Goebbels and to Hitler personally over the phone who assured him that he had safely survived the plot to assassinate him. Remer was then promoted to the rank of General and given full power to crush the coup and restore order in Berlin.

On the evening of the 20th, Remer accordingly moved his battalion from the government district and ordered his troops to storm the Home Army headquarters to arrest the coup plotters.

Later in the war he became the commander of the Führer-Begleit Division, and survived the destruction of this unit in 1945.

In 1950 he became Deputy Chairman of the neo-Nazi Socialist Reich Party. In this position he delivered scathing attacks on the 'traitors of July 20th' and characterised their legacy as a 'stain on the shield of honour of the German officer corps' who had 'stabbed the German Army in the back.'

In 1952 he was sentenced to three months in prison for 'collective libel against the German Resistance', and fled Germany for Egypt. For the rest of his life he remained a dedicated Nazi, and in October 1992 was arrested in Germany and sentenced to 22 months in prison for publishing neo-Nazi propaganda and denying the existence of the Holocaust. He died in 1997.

DIETRICH VON SAUCKEN

Born in 1892 von Saucken was Panzer-Corps *Grossdeutschland* commander in the final stages of the war, prior to his hurried appointment as commanding officer of the Second Army. He had a varied career in the Wehrmacht, typifying those fortunate to survive six years of war. He had been CO of 2nd Reserve Regiment

1937–40, commanded 4th Schützen-Brigade 1940–41, was general officer commanding 4th Panzer Division 1941–42, commandant Mobile Troops School 1942–43, general officer commanding 4th Panzer Division 1943–44, deputy general officer commanding III Panzer Corps 1944, general officer commanding XXXIX Panzer Corps 1944, general officer commanding Panzer Corps *Grossdeutschland* 1944–45, and general officer commanding Second Army, Eastern Front 1945. He died in 1980.

Below: Carried shoulder high to his assault gun, Hauptmann Frantz, commander of the Assault Artillery Detachment of Infantry Division *Grossdeutschland*, celebrates the award of the Oak Leaves to his Knight's Cross, June 1943.

Commanders of *Grossdeutschland*

Name	CO From	To	Comments
Generalmajor Wilhelm Stockhausen	1/9/39	31/7/41	GD raised as Inf Regt (mot). Stockhausen promoted from Oberst
Generalleutnant Walter Hoernlein	1/8/41	31/1/44	GD becomes Inf Div (mot) 1/4/42. 'Papa' Hoernlein promoted from Oberst
Generalleutnant Hermann Balck	3/4/43	30/6/43	Temporary commander
Generalleutnant Hasso-Eckard von Manteuffel	1/2/44	31/8/44	Promoted to command Fifth Panzer Army
Generalmajor Karl Lorenz	1/9/44	30/11/44	GD becomes Pz Corps
General Dietrich von Saucken	1/12/44	31/1/45	Promoted to command Second Army
General (Pz) Georg Jauer	1/2/45	5/45	Surrendered in various locations
General Willi Langkeit	3/2/45	21/4/45	Commanded Kurmark Division; destroyed by Russians. Langkeit promoted from Oberst
Generalmajor Ernst-Otto Remer	20/7/44	21/4/45	Führer-Begleit-Regiment formed; later (27/1/44) becomes a Brigade; later still (30/1/45) becomes a division. Remer promoted from Oberst, surrendered to Russians

ASSESSMENT

Right: Dr Joseph Goebbels, the Reich Propaganda Minister, was created 'patron' of Panzer Regiment *Grossdeutschland*. He is shown here being greeted by the Regimental Commander with Panzer IIs in the background.

Below right: A battalion commander offers up a light to one of his wounded grenadiers.

It is difficult to assess the effect of an individual unit on a battle, there being so many factors to take into consideration, and well nigh impossible to judge the effect it has on a war, particularly when that unit was on the losing side. When taking account of *Grossdeutschland's* combat record it is possible to state that the unit did play a decisive role in many of the actions in which it fought and can thereby justly be considered one of the finest infantry formations of World War II.

At the beginning of the war the unit was four battalions strong, and by the end of the conflict *Grossdeutschland* members were fighting in four divisions, in several hastily formed combat groups and other smaller groups. In the early years the process of expanding the unit was a direct result of the Wehrmacht's desire to combat the strength and prestige of the SS, but by 1945 it was a desperate measure to bolster the flagging strength of the army.

In the battle of France, the unit showed for the first time what it was capable of under fire, battling over the Meuse at Sedan to establish a vital bridgehead for the Panzers to sweep through to Channel, and then successfully resisting the Allied counter-attacks on the thin spearhead, despite losing almost a quarter of its strength in the western offensive.

It was if anything stronger for this experience by the opening of the offensive in the east, where it remained for the rest of the war. In the first weeks of the campaign GD was part of the spearhead that made the lightning advance to Smolensk and in the first year of the campaign GD was assigned to many units, often to support assaults on major objectives. By the end of the year it was at the gates of Moscow. In 1942 the regiment was expanded to division size and held the Russian advance at Bolkhov. On the first day of the Caucasus offensive, GD was at the spearhead of an advance that broke through on the Tim. Through the summer it fought at points along the whole line from the Manych River to Rzhev, and was instrumental in the capture of Rostov and the Maikop oilfields.

As it grew in size and stature, so did the expectations of what it could achieve, and during the defensive battles that followed the victories of 1941–42 GD was constantly on the move, transferred from north to south to shore up the weak points in the German lines or else to hold back the tide of the Soviet advance. At Rzhev, from the middle of August 1942 it fought almost continually to hold the city. By the end of a savage year of fighting and despite losing many men, especially first in February and then in December, the unit had grown in stature and never lost its cohesion.

It soon earned the nickname 'The Fire Brigade' because of its almost legendary ability to stamp out crises as they flared up. Nonetheless, the dangerous work of the 'Fire Brigade' took a heavy toll on its men, and increasingly courage alone could

Right: The face of war: festooned with ammunition belts this young grenadier, complete with machine gun and dressed in winter clothing, prepares to move off, April 1943.

not compensate for the overwhelming superiority of the Soviet forces. Again, during 1943, the unit was active across the whole sector of the central and southern fronts, fighting heavy defensive battles and launching counter-attacks. In defence the division proved as skillful as in attack, its desperate defence and heroic counter-attack around Byelgorod in early 1943 being of particular note.

In the thwarted Citadel offensive *Grossdeutschland* was thrown against one of the heaviest and best defended sectors of the Russian line, yet was able to make some local breakthroughs. Around Karachev, in July and August 1943, it thwarted an attempt to encircle the German Eleventh Army with skillful counter-attacks, and at Akhtyrka held up the Soviet steamroller during the retreat, preventing the envelopment of Army Group South. At the Kremenchug bridgehead over the Dnieper in September, it performed heroically again.

1944 was another year of defence, counter-attack and movement, on southern, central and northern fronts. Something of the reputation of the division, and its status among the leadership, can be gleaned from the number of units that carried its name. In the critical battles on the northern front *Grossdeutschland* again distinguished itself, fighting to prevent the Soviet breakthrough to the Baltic and waging a desperate battle to cover the retreat of the German armies through the Memel bridgehead

In 1945, its ranks severely depleted, the corps fought almost to the last man to save Berlin from capture, and its part in delaying the Soviet advance is perhaps part of the reason that Germany was not swamped under the Red tide.

The fact that *Grossdeutschland* was able to survive as a unit during this long period of attrition was in part due to the quality of the officers and men, who were selected from the fittest and ablest recruits. As with all German divisions, *Grossdeutschland* maintained training depots for the reception and integration of replacements instead of sending them piecemeal into the front lines. As the war ground on, combat units were reduced in size and veterans were carefully distributed to form the nucleus for strong primary groups. Strenuous measures were taken to ensure that junior leaders possessed experience and competence; where an American infantry company might boast 150 soldiers and four or five inexperienced lieutenants, a German company might carry 50 or 70 soldiers on its rolls but with a single seasoned officer in command. Importantly, the corps of non-commissioned officers was not diluted to replace officer losses, which might have destroyed the cohesion of the smaller units, and lengthy NCO training courses were continued right up until the end of the war.

Throughout the war *Grossdeutschland* was hamstrung by its own success, which often led to a gross overestimation of its capabilities and propelled it again and again into the fiercest battles. In the closing actions of the war, fighting in disparate units against the Soviet invader, the corps literally fought to the death. Panzer-Grenadier-Division *Grossdeutschland* alone suffered nearly 17,000 casualties. In its short history *Grossdeutschland* tirelessly, professionally and often heroically fought under conditions that would have finished most other military units.

REFERENCE

INTERNET SITES:

http://www.geocities.com/Pentagon/3620/
Achtung Panzer!
Interesting site with very detailed information on German armour.
Great pictures of preserved machines, particularly SPWs.

http://www.feldgrau.com/
This is probably the most comprehensive site currently on the
Web dealing with the German Army before and during World
War II. Well-written and researched, and an intriguing in-
depth interview with a *Grossdeutschland* veteran, too.

http://www.geocities.com/gd7silent/
The group re-enacts the engagements of the 7th Company of
Grossdeutschland. Lots of info, pictures and links to other re-
enactment groups, and still growing. (e-mail:
feldpost@grossdeutschland.com)

http://users.ids.net/~bclauss/index.htm
Homepage of a group of 3. Panzer-Grenadier-Division re-enactors.
Also has links to the 43. Sturm-Pionier re-enactment group.

http://www.angelfire.com/rant/grossdeutschland/home.html
Another US re-enactor site.

http://ourworld.compuserve.com/homepages/hallg/frame1.htm
A Living History UK re-enactment site.

http://www.multimania.com/dday44/uniforme/uniforme.htm
French-language site with some interesting pictures of uniforms,
including a *Grossdeutschland* trooper.

http://www.tankclub.agava.ru/sign/sign.shtml
Russian-language site with excellent illustrations of the tactical
signs of the German Army.

http://www.generals.dk
This is an private project trying to provide biographical data on the army generals of World War II, including many German generals.

http://www.eliteforcesofthethirdreich.com/
Useful information on PKGD and associated units

http://grossdeutschland.freehosting.net/index.htm
This excellent site provides information for game players but has much for the enthusiast including a full examination of vehicle markings at http://grossdeutschland.freehosting.net/vehicle.htm.

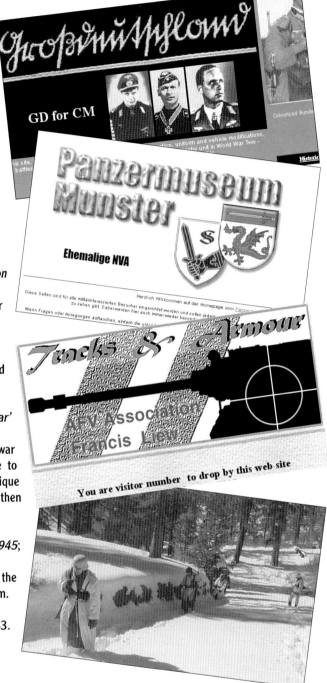

BIBLIOGRAPHY

Bender, R. & Odegard, W.; *Panzertruppe—Uniforms, Organisation and History*; Bender, 1980.
Panzer formations 1935–45, Panzer uniforms and insignia, Panzer markings and camouflage are all given in detail.

Culver, B. & Murphy, B.; *Panzer Colours—Vol. 1*.
170 illustrations with 69 full-colour plates provide a detailed account of German armour during WWII.

Delaney, J.; *The Blitzkrieg Campaigns. Germany's 'Lighting War' Strategy in Action*; Arms and Armour, 1996.
Describes the origins of the strategy developed during the interwar years — a strong, co-ordinated, mobile land and air offensive to surprise and envelop an unprepared enemy. Studies how this technique was used during the advances into Poland, Belgium and France then Russia.

Engelmann, Joachim; *German Artillery in World War II 1939-1945*; Schiffer Publishing, 1995. English translation.
This volume of photographs presents a detailed look into the operations, action and everyday life of the Wehrmacht artillery arm.

Erickson, John; *The Road to Stalingrad & The Road to Berlin*; 1983.
Weidenfeld and Nicolson/Westview Press, 1983 & 1984
A two-volume definitive study of Stalin's war with Germany.

Efomichenko, Major General; *The Red Army*; Hutchinson, n.d.
Studies the development of The Soviet Army and its exploits from June 1941. Analyses how the Red Army foiled Hitler's plans by pushing back the Axis forces from the Volga and the Caucasus into the Reich itself.

Forty, George, & Duncan, John; *The Fall of France—Disaster in the West 1939–1940*; Guild Publishing, 1990
A pictorial analysis of how the Panzer divisions defeated France within six weeks.

Fuller, J.F.C.; *The Second World War 1939-1945*; Meredith, 1968
This was the first comprehensive strategic and tactical history of the war to be written, and stirred controversy. The book has sixty specially drawn maps and diagrams.

Glantz, David; *From the Don to the Dnieper*;
Illustrations with detailed maps are included in this analysis of Red Army operations – eight vital months of struggle that finally ended Hitler's Blitzkrieg against the USSR.

Grechko, Andrei; *Battle for the Caucasus*;
A Marshal of the Soviet Union pays tribute to his Red Army troops who withstood and repelled the Nazi advance during the battle for the Caucasus, July 1942 – October 1942, a victory that helped change the course of WWII.

Guderian, Heinz; *Panzer Leader*; Michael Joseph, 1952.
The autobiography of the famous German general.

Hoffschmidt, E. J. & Tantum, W. H.; *Combat Weapons, Volume 1 German*; WE Inc, 1968
An illustrated encyclopedia of all German tanks, artillery, small arms, mortars, rockets and grenades.

Jentz, Thomas L.; *Panzertruppen* Vol 1 1933–42, Vol 2 1943–45; Schiffer, 1996
Volume 1 is a complete guide to the creation, organisation and combat employment of Germany's tank force. Volume 2 describes how, when forced on to the defensive, the Panzer formations became expert at counter attacks. The detail is all drawn from original German records.

Kershaw, Robert; *War without Garlands—Operation Barbarossa 1941/42*; Ian Allan Publishing, 2000.
Excellent analysis of the early stages of Germany's war with Russia with plenty of eyewitness accounts.

Kriegsberichter
A bi-monthly magazine for students of the German armed forces in World War II, published in California by Erich Craciun.

Kurowski Franz; *Knights of the Wehrmacht*;
A study of the Knight's Cross holders.

Lucas, James; *Germany's Elite Panzer Force*; Macdonald and Jane's, 1979
A history of the *Grossdeutschland* formation's historic rise from an infantry regiment to a Panzer corps in six years.

Lucas, James; *War on the Eastern Front—The German Soldier in Russia*; Jane's, 1979
An account of the war against the Soviet Union from the German angle.

Lucas, James; T*he Last Year of the German Army May 1944—May 1945*; BCA, 1994
A complete study of structural changes made to try and overcome the army's depletion and an insight into some of its last battles.

McLean, Donald B. (Ed); *German Infantry Weapons Vol 1*; Normount Armament Co, 1967
Originally published in 1943 to assist Allied commanders, details the design and construction of weapons and their ammunition.

Messenger, Charles; *The Art of Blitzkrieg*; Ian Allan, 1976
Studies Blitzkrieg's evolution as a technique of war and describes how Hitler used the theory so effectively.

Metelmann, Henry; *Through Hell for Hitler*; Patrick Stephens, 1990
A dramatic account of fighting with the Wehrmacht in Russia.

Mitcham, S.A. Jnr.; *Hitler's Legions*; Leo Cooper, 1985
The organisation and technical aspects of the German divisions are described. Every part of the army is covered.

Nafziger, George F.; *The German Order of Battle Panzers and Artillery in World War II*; Greenhill Books, 1999.
Defeinitive orders of battle.

Pallud, Jean Paul; *Blitzkrieg in the West – Then and Now*; After the Battle, 1991
Fully illustrated. Then and now photographs show how Germany, in just sixty days, caused France to capitulate during 1940.

Piekalkiewicz, Janusz; *Operation Citadel*; Presidio, 1987
A complete illustrated analysis of the Battles of Kursk and Orel which shattered Nazi ambitions in Russia.

Sajer, Guy; *The Forgotten Soldier*; Harper and Row, 1971. English translation
A German soldier, drafted into *Grossdeutschland* in 1942 despite being of French/German descent, provides a vivid chronicle of the faceless anonymity of total war in the endless bitter wastes of Russia.

Scheibert, Horst & Culver, Bruce (Ed); *Panzer Grenadier Division Gross Deutschland*; Squadron/Signal, 1987
An excellent pictorial reference work on the *Grossdeutschland* units.

Above: The crew of a *Hornisse* (Hornet) anti-tank gun awaits orders. Designed to carry a 88mm PAK 43/1 on a Panzer III or IV chassis, the Hornisse was introduced into combat in late 1943.

Glossary

Abteilung	Battalion
Armee	Army
Armeegruppe	Army Group
Artillerie	Artillery
Aufklärung	Recce
Ausbildung	Training
Bataillon	Battalion
Begleit	Escort
Einheiten	Units
Ersatz	Replacement
Fallschirmjäger	Parachute troops
Feldersatz	Field replacement
Flak	AA gun
Geschütz	Gun
Grenadier	Rifleman
Heer	German Army
Heerestruppen	Independent army units
Infanterie	Infantry
Kampfgruppe	Battle group
Kavallerie	Cavalry
Kompanie	Company
Kraftfahrpark	Maintenance depot
Landser	Line infantryman
Lehr	Training
Leichte	Light
Litzen	Collar patch
LSSAH	*Liebstandarte* SS Adolf Hitler (1st SS Panzer Division)
Luftwaffe	German Air Force
Motorisiert	Motorised
NSDAP	Nationalsozialistische Deutsche Arbeiterpatei —Nazi Party
Nachrichten	Signals
Nebelwerfer	Grenade launcher (multi-barrel)
OKH	Army High Command (*Oberkommando des Heeres*)
OKW	Armed Forces High Command (*Oberkommando der Wehrmacht*)
Pak	Anti-tank gun (*Panzer Abwehr Kanone*)
Panzergrenadier	Armed infantry
Panzerjäger	Anti-tank infantry
PIAT	Projectile, Infantry, Anti-Tank
Pionier	Engineer
PzKpfw	*Panzerkampwagen* (tank/AFV)
RAD	Reichsarbeitsdienst (National Labour Service)
Sanität	Medical
Schirmmütze	Peaked cap
Schütze	Rifleman
Schwer	Heavy
SdKfz	*Sonderkraftfahrzeug* (special purpose vehicle)
Stab	Staff (HQ)
Stahlhelm	Steel helmet
Stamm	Cadre
Stellung	Position/static
StuG	Sturmgeschutz (assault gun)
Sturmgeschütz	Assault Gun
Truppe	Troop
VGD	Volksgrenadier division
Versorgungstruppen	Service troops
Wache	Guard
Waffenfarben	Colour on collars etc, Denoting branch of Service
Wehrkreis	War district
Wehrmacht	German armed forces
Zug	Platoon

Abbreviations

AA	Anti-aircraft
ADC	Aide de camp
Arty	Artillery
Atk	Anti-tank
Bn	Battalion
BR	Brandenburg
Brig	Brigade
Bty	Battery
Col	Column
Coy	Company
Det	Detachment
Engr	Engineer
FB	Führer Begleit (escort), Bn (Bn), R (Regt), B (Brigade), D (Div)
FGD	Führer Grenadier Division
GD	Grossdeutschland
Hy	Heavy
IDGD	Infantry Division Grossdeutschland
IRGD	Infantry Regiment Grossdeutschland
le FH	leichte Feldhaubitze (light field gun)
Lt	Lieutenant; light
Maint	Maintenance
MC	Motorcycle
Mor	Mortar
Mot	Motorised
Mtrel	Materiel
Pl	Platoon
PzBefWag	Panzerbefehls-wagen (armed comd vehicle)
PzGr	Panzergrenadier
PzJr	Panzerjäger
QM	Quartermaster
Recce	Reconnaissance
RA	Royal Artillery
RHQ	Regimental HQ
Sect	Section
Sig	Signals
SP	Self-propelled
Tac	Tactical
Tk	Tank
Veh	Vehicle
WH	Wehrmacht Heer

INDEX